# THE SHAMAN'S GUIDE TO
# HEALING CRYSTALS

## Making Medicine Bags ◆ Using Energy Stones

# Amy Zerner and Monte Farber

## STERLING

New York / London
www.sterlingpublishing.com

HEALING CRYSTALS
The Shaman's Guide to Making Medicine Bags
and Using Energy Stones

Text and art copyright © Amy Zerner & Monte Farber 2010
All photos copyright © Monte Farber 2010
This edition copyright © Zerner/Farber Editions 2010

Published by:
Sterling Publishing Co., Inc.
387 Park Avenue South
New York, NY 10016-8810

For information, address
The Enchanted World of Amy Zerner & Monte Farber
Post Office Box 2299, East Hampton, NY 11937 USA
E-mail: info@TheEnchantedWorld.com
Website: www.TheEnchantedWorld.com

Library of Congress Cataloging-in-Publication Data
available on request.
ISBN: 978-1-4027-7085-2
First U.S. edition published 2010
9 8 7 6 5 4 3 2 1

Graphic design by Rose Sheifer-Wright

For information about custom editions, special sales,
premium and corporate purchases, please contact
Sterling Special Sales Department at 800-805-5489 or
specialsales@sterlingpub.com

Printed in China through Colorcraft Ltd, Hong Kong .

For entertainment purposes only.

133
ze

# CONTENTS

# Introduction

**Healing Crystals:**
**A Shaman's Guide to Making Medicine Bags**
**and Using Energy Stones.**

*The Shamanic forces of the mind and planet can be harnessed for the service of wisdom and compassion, each tradition enhanced by the perspectives and methods of the other.*

—His Holiness, the Dalai Lama

If you think that sounds like there's a lot packed into this book, you're right. In its pages you are going to encounter some of the most fascinating, useful, and empowering information we have ever shared with our readers, information that can actually help you change your life at a profound level by changing the way you look at the world.

Everything in this book is based on the latest scientific discoveries but filtered through our experience as the authors of more than forty books on ancient spiritual wisdom teachings. As people who try to keep up with the advances in our culture—yes, we're optimists and think our culture is advancing—it seems to us that the next round of miraculous technological advancements is going to occur because of the work of the many theoretical scientists who are now putting forth theories about how the world works. These theories are, to our ears, remarkably similar to the very core beliefs of these ancient wisdom teachings, and nowhere is this more evident then in the astonishing discoveries and practical applications surrounding crystals.

We realize that you are anxious to get to work using your healing crystals and making your medicine bags, but please do not skip this introduction. It is designed to take you from your present level of understanding about crystals to the level you need to be on to get the most from *Healing Crystals*.

As the Chinese philosopher Lao Tzu wrote, "The journey of a thousand miles begins beneath one's feet." Before you can take even one step toward learning how to use healing crystals to change your life for the better or to make medicine bags to carry and protect them, it is crucial that you are first grounded in the confident stillness that comes from knowing the subject thoroughly. Join us now on an amazing journey to the place where science and shamanism meet, a place where magic happens all the time. As you will soon see, that place is a lot closer than you might imagine, close to where your feet are right now....

# What Is a Crystal?

The Earth is literally covered in crystals. The word *crystal* comes from the Greek *krystallos*, a derivative of the Greek word for *frozen*.

The continental crust we walk upon is composed primarily of rocks known as *granitic*, or quartz rich, like granite. Under the oceans, the surface of the Earth is composed of rocks that are called *basaltic*, also a crystal-rich material that is formed when the Earth's mantel liquefies and cools, as it did when it formed approximately four billion years ago and since that time whenever volcanoes have spewed molten lava.

Where continent and ocean meet are even more crystals, the beaches of sand (chemical name *silica*), which are crystalline in structure. Silica and *bauxite*, the name given to aluminum ore, are the two most prevalent substances on the surface of our lovely Earth, which might more accurately be called the planet Crystal!

Many of the crystal gemstones we focus on in this book occur naturally in the Earth, formed from the crystallized deposits of mineral-infused (aqueous) liquids over many thousands and often millions of years, or sometimes relatively quickly from the heat and pressure of volcanic activity.

To the average person, the term *crystal* refers to expensive glassware, salt and sugar, and cut and polished gemstones. A smaller percentage of people know about the relationship of crystals and the "New Age" movement or large crystals and clusters, each one born of and taken from a *geode*, many of which sit on coffee tables and office desks as beautiful and often colorful decorations.

The definition scientists used to accept for what makes a crystal a crystal was any solid whose atoms, ions, or molecules formed a single, regularly repeating internal unit of structure—such as a triangle, square, pentagon, octagon—but in all three dimensions of space. As technology has progressed and allowed scientists to see and think more clearly, the definition of what precisely constitutes a crystal has begun to sound more and more like the centuries-old wisdom teachings of indigenous peoples that are at the heart of this book.

It was in 1982 that the old definition of a crystal was found to be inexact. Scientist

Dan Shechtman discovered that there exist *quasicrystals*, substances with crystal-like individual arrays of atoms that are not regularly repeated. The term *crystal* was redefined by him to mean "any solid having an essentially discrete diffraction diagram."

This definition is a remarkable statement. A crystal is now any substance that possesses, at the atomic or molecular level, the ability to diffract (bend the path of) not only precisely targeted beams of electrons or X-rays in a regular, distinctive, and repeatable pattern, but light, too. A crystal is a crystal because it can rearrange photons of light in a coherent, repeatable pattern. Anyone who works with crystals is a light worker, by definition.

*Light worker* is a term used colloquially by those of us who have dedicated our lives to helping others help themselves. We like to think that we are a powerful force for good and will help to reduce the darkness that always threatens to engulf even our best efforts, though we know well that doing what is right does not guarantee that things will turn out the way we want them to. Writing this book has helped me to become even more optimistic about the power each of us has to change the world. There is a scientific as well as a spiritual basis for what we are proposing here in the pages of *Healing Crystals*: We each have allies of immense power in the form of our healing crystals and our medicine bags.

To begin my case for this, consider how crucial crystal power is to many of the crowning technological achievements of modern society. The most obvious example is the ability of electronic devices that contain specially shaped crystals—often rubies—to diffract, internally concentrate, and reflect light in a coherent beam able to travel distances large and small to deliver information or even destructive forces in heretofore miraculous ways. We call that device a laser, and whole books have been written about how they have changed our world. Additionally, a crystal's ability to modulate and control electronic signals and frequencies of all kinds enables radio and television signals, computer chips, and virtually all of our modern communication technologies.

In the pages of *Healing Crystals* we suggest and attempt to prove that crystals have even greater powers. We believe that they can help people focus and direct their intention to work their will on the world. This is the essence of magic, but it is easy to see that almost all of what we experience daily would have been considered magic less than a century ago.

Scanning electron microscopes, which use crystals to control their beams of energy, reveal that everything solid is composed of atoms, which are mainly space. We are, each of us, a miraculous composition of atomic and electrical forces that are also undoubtedly affected by the native properties of crystals. Amy and I believe that the miraculous powers of crystals, already discovered and confirmed by science and exemplified by the immense power of lasers, suggest that crystals also have the ability to diffract, internally concentrate, and reflect *all* the energies that surround us, including the spiritual forces that support and sustain our essentially atomic human existence.

This is one of the main reasons why it seems to us that science has arrived at the ancient shamanic description of our true nature, what is commonly called our *spirit*. It can also be called our vital life force, our *aura* or our *etheric body*. (*Ether* was the medieval alchemists' name for pure energy, unfettered by form, like the *E* for energy in Einstein's famous equation $E = mc^2$!) This energetic body was known as our *chi* by the Chinese and our *prana* by the Hindus.

Since crystals have the ability to transmit, transform, increase, or step down the energy that passes through them, it seems logical to us that crystals may be able to act as the intermediary between our individual chi-aura-spirit energies—for that is what we are in essence—and the limitless energy of Creation, what the Native Americans call "the Great Spirit." The goal then is to learn how to use our crystals to attune ourselves to the vibrational frequencies that can heal us.

We believe that each crystal gemstone has its own vibrational powers that can assist with our attunement to healing energies if we can train ourselves to be as clear as, well, crystal when we do so. We further believe that the special vibrations of our gemstones can be accessed by using a process that incorporates our intention to help support the energy of the cells in our body and thus may promote healing.

To us, this ancient technique that uses the healing power of crystals integrated with our own desire is like an Internet search engine, like Google, but on a spiritual level, translating the energy of our intention and requests to the universe and receiving the healing blessings and any other answers that the universe sends back. This now makes sense to you (I hope!), but is it any wonder that using crystals for healing sounds far-fetched to those who don't understand even the scientifically accepted capabilities of crystals? It is like describing Google to the head librarian of the U.S. Library of Congress as recently as 1990—it sounds impossible!

We have chosen the fifteen Master Healing Crystals to work with in this book, as they are easy to find and have served us well during our decades of working with them. *Healing Crystals* offers a spiritual practice to help restore wholeness, balance, and health to the mind, body, and spirit—it is safe, easy, and effective. Any form of disharmony in our lives, whether on the spiritual, mental, or physical level, can cause disturbances in our lives and in our health. Using the gentle, transformative qualities of focusing our intention to restore ourselves and our surroundings to harmony and amplifying and directing our intention with crystal energy have helped us in our own lives many times.

Healing crystals are born from the body of Mother Earth, sometimes over millions of years and sometimes in an instant during times of great heat, light, and volatility. We have come to believe that they are able to absorb, contain, and transmit the ancient wisdom and cosmic vibrations of universal consciousness. To us, there is nothing more elemental and yet mystical than a natural crystal—they are powerful psychic tools of protection and enlightenment—and we have quite a collection of them. They tell us their stories, they listen to what we have to say to them, and, when we ask them clearly for help, they help us as best they can.

So those who say that crystals are New Age are more correct than they know, for without the scientific application of the seemingly miraculous properties of crystals, life in the twenty-first century would be quite similar to that in the nineteenth century and not the logical, exponential extension of the twentieth century's technological advances that we enjoy today.

We believe that when we work with crystals' essential ability, their ability to work with light, these seemingly lifeless stones can help us to find our personal definition of enlightenment. We have created *Healing Crystals* with the intention that it will help you to improve your life on the spiritual, mental, and physical planes of existence, thereby allowing you to share your new successful way of living with those you care about. This will happen when you come to realize that you can use your crystals to become a modern-day shaman.

# What Is a Shaman?

The word *shaman* comes from the language of the Tungus of Siberia. It came into use in English by way of Russia. The word originated from *öamán*, which is the Turkic-Tungus word meaning "he or she who knows." Therefore, *shaman* means a wise sage, someone who knows. Another translation gives the fundamental meaning as "one who is moved, raised," which also addresses the principle characteristics of the shaman, which is that he or she has been raised up or elevated—an exalted member of the tribe.

The term *shaman* has grown in colloquial usage to include traditions outside of the original Siberian cultures from which it originated. In *Healing Crystals*, we use it to describe the men and women in any culture who are responsible for tuning in to the "other world" to help heal people's physical, mental, and spiritual conditions.

In general, a shaman's tasks include:

- Restoring wellness
- Purifying energy
- Mending discord
- Improving relationships
- Interpreting visions
- Giving meaning to events

A shaman is a person who interacts with both the normal, everyday world and the unseen world of spirits. The ideal shaman unites the roles of healer, visionary, counselor, and prophet. Shamans are individuals with the ability to work with Earth energies and to see and interpret visions for the benefit of their tribes. Many shamans claim to be able to predict the future and interpret signs. They claim to see signs all around them, in the ordinary and the extraordinary, and hear the voices from the spirit and animal realms.

In the past, the ability to be considered a shaman was restricted to rare individuals who were chosen for the role, enduring rigorous training and constant teaching by the shamans who came before them. However, the vibration of human life on our planet has obviously speeded up to a degree once thought impossible. We believe that vibrational increase and the almost overwhelming amount of information learned by even a moderately educated person brings an intelligent, open-minded person of today very close to the level of awareness possessed by the shamans of yesterday. All that is necessary for shamanic wisdom and power to be attained is for a person to change the way he or she looks at the world, guided by the wise ones who have come before us.

Amy and I have studied and practiced our art and our craft for decades, working to bring the essence of shamanic wisdom to a wide range of people who also seek enchantment, enlightenment, and self-empowerment. We are proud to say that we now have more than two million copies of our published works in print around the world in fourteen languages. As our friend, the great Mayan elder and master shaman Hunbatz Men, told me when I met with him in Mexico's Yucatán Peninsula, asking for and receiving his blessing of our shamanic work, "Yes. We have got to make thousands of shamans now. We are entering sacred times."

As shamans often do, we humbly ask the Great Spirit for help in our endeavors. In this case, we pray that Hunbatz Men's potent blessing extends to you and your efforts to work with *Healing Crystals*, to help you get in touch with your "inner shaman," the part of you that knows beyond doubt that there is more to life than meets the eye. The fact that you were drawn to and are reading this book shows that you, too, suspect this to be true and are willing to investigate the facts with an open mind and the desire to know the truth. You are both wise and in illustrious company, for the healing power of crystals is not some idle flight of fancy; it is a scientific fact proven by one of the greatest scientists of all time.

# Marcel Vogel,
## Twentieth-Century Shaman and Crystal Healer

Although there are now relatively few scientists who would immediately understand and respect the work of shamans like Hunbatz Men or our work, Amy and I have the greatest respect for science and scientists. We know the truth of what we speak because we see it work so powerfully in our own lives, and so we are confident and content and do not need the approval of others before we can respect them and their work. We believe that scientists are to Western civilization what shamans are to their tribes.

In our opinion, one of the greatest scientist-shamans of the twentieth century—on a par with Albert Einstein—was a man by the name of Marcel Vogel (1917–1991). Vogel was an American, a senior scientist with IBM for twenty-seven years, the pioneering inventor and patent holder of numerous world-changing devices including the liquid crystal diodes (LCDs) in computers, flat-screen TVs, and all kinds of electronic displays, the magnetic coating that enables your computer's hard drive to store information, Day-Glo paints and black light, and many more inventions of practical use.

After retiring from IBM in 1984, Vogel spent the last seventeen years of his life researching the relationship between quartz crystals and water, which he found also had the ability to store information; water has "memory," like the coating of your hard drive does. To do this, he created his own laboratory, Psychic Research, Inc. The lab was dedicated to the study of subtle forces and energies that radiate from the bodies of living forms, also known as auras. It was his intent to measure these forces and formulate a system of identification for these energies, which have most often been labeled and dismissed as "metaphysical," a word that means "beyond the physical."

Marcel Vogel's projects included the following:

1. The structuring of water for purification purposes
2. The structuring of wines to rapidly age them
3. The measurement of energy fields around a crystal
4. The therapeutic application of crystals and crystal devices

It is important to remember that it was Marcel Vogel, a scientist of unquestioned importance, who discovered that pure quartz crystal displayed all the characteristics of the behavior of light itself, calling it "enlightened matter." This was no crackpot, but a man with a consistent track record of making scientific breakthroughs of societal importance. He contributed greatly to technologies that help crystals modulate carrier waves and transmit energy frequencies into space and back to our most common home devices, such as lasers, radios, television sets, radar, satellites, cell phones, computers, and a number of other electronic devices used on a daily basis. It is hard to imagine our world without the inventive genius of twentieth-century scientist-shaman Marcel Vogel.

# What Is a Healing Crystal?

Vogel was a scientist who was also deeply religious, a phenomenon that is more common than you might think. When first presented with various theories about the "secret" life of plants, which he also studied, and the healing power of crystals—things that sounded like a contradiction of his religious beliefs—he was very skeptical, as every scientist and, for that matter, every nonscientist should be. As the Bible's 146th Psalm says, "Put not thy faith in princes." Even so, he gave them a fair hearing, in the tradition of British naturalist Sir Thomas Huxley, who famously said, "I'm too much a skeptic not to believe that anything's possible."

Now that you know who Marcel Vogel was, you are ready to read a few of the many things that he wrote about crystals in a different light than if you were to simply read them not knowing the great mind that produced these words and swore by their accuracy:

> *The crystal is a neutral object whose inner structure exhibits a state of perfection and balance. . . . Like a laser, it radiates energy in a coherent, highly concentrated form, and this energy may be transmitted into objects or people at will. . . . With proper training, a healer using a crystal can release negative thought forms which have taken shape as disease patterns.*

Any person with such deeply held beliefs—about religion or, for that matter, anything else—has an easier time focusing his or her intention in a laserlike manner than most other people would. So those who can easily focus their attention and their intention while working

*A crystal is an assemblage of molecules that form a unit cell, a consciousness, a soul. It takes your program and draws to itself the replication of its image.*

— Marcel Vogel

with a crystal can expect to accomplish far more than those who can concentrate only with effort. The good news for those whose ability to concentrate needs improvement is that following the instructions here in *Healing Crystals* can help you do just that.

This type of focus is a valuable skill for the successful use of healing crystals and for many other areas of life. Perhaps that was why Marcel Vogel, one of the few senior scientists at IBM to have no college degree, was able to be so successful in business and get such remarkable, repeatable results in energy work with crystals. He even developed specially cut Vogel Crystals, authorized examples of which are still made today (beware of imitations).

When Marcel Vogel discovered for himself that the energies of mind could affect matter, he then went into serious scientific research. Here, in brief, are a few of his fundamental discoveries regarding the thought energies of mind and crystals, which he also called "Telephones to God."

- Our intentions can be projected regardless of time and space.

- Quartz crystals can amplify, store, and transfer these energies of thought.

- The inhaling and exhaling of breath is connected to the receiving and transmitting of thought information.

- Breath, when exhaled through the nostrils in a rapid burst, has the greatest degree of projecting thought.

- The structuring by thought into a crystal can be transferred into water by spinning the water around the crystal in a right-hand spiral tube of seven turns, leaving the water structured with that thought pattern that was programmed within the crystal.

- We are patterned after that which created us, and therefore we create. Everything hinges around suggestion; as we believe so we create.

We all owe Marcel Vogel a debt that can be repaid only by taking to heart and sharing with those we care about his equally world-changing discoveries about the healing property of crystals. When we do, we not only honor his memory but become his helpers, increasing the understanding and use of the concepts and positive changes to which he devoted his life. He was a true shaman and we are proud to dedicate *Healing Crystals* to him.

# What Is Your Medicine?

At some point in their training, shamans of indigenous cultures must embark upon a vision quest, an often perilous journey into the wilderness to purify themselves so that a vision of their special mission in life may be given to them, often through the intermediary of a "power animal," whose appearance coincides with this revelation. The shaman must pass through the fires of self-examination and self-transformation, and into the darkness of the shadow side of negativity that we all possess, emerging from this inner journey a stronger and wiser person. As Lao Tzu also wrote in his seminal work of philosophy, *The Book of Tao*, "He who overcomes others is great. He who overcomes himself is greatest."

No matter what it takes, shamans must heal themselves if they and their wisdom are to be useful to others in their own journeys from suffering to healing. During a vision quest, shamans are alone, fasting, and oftentimes have to endure terrible privations in order to prepare themselves to face the ultimate enemy—fear, starting with the fear of dying. The shamans' goal is to encounter themselves completely, and by facing and ultimately embracing their fears as wise teachers, they come back to their tribes as fully integrated humans, better able to serve the spiritual needs of their people and help them find their individual "medicine" so that they, too, can be healed physically, mentally, and spiritually. This is why shamans are also called "medicine men."

All shamans look at life as a continuous process of healing. This is what makes them driven to teach those who look to them for guidance the importance of finding one's "medicine," anything and everything that will help us heal the physical, mental, and emotional wounds we all carry and help us to live our lives to the full. Any belief system that is predicated upon the idea of the spiritual energy in nature interacting constantly with our "ordinary" world and endeavors to strengthen the direct link between each person and the ultimate source of his or her being is essentially shamanistic.

# What Is a Healing Crystal Medicine Bag?

In most every culture, shamans embarking on a vision quest and other spiritual healers honor the tradition of their ancestors and teachers by carrying and using something known as a medicine bag. Medicine bags are various-sized pouches containing sacred objects, especially crystals, bones, feathers, and stones, but they can carry any small object of significance to the shaman.

Amulet bags have been made in African nations, for the indigenous peoples throughout the Americas, and in Europe and Asia, too. It is rare to find a practitioner of any nature religion, such as Wicca, without his or her personal medicine bag.

When used with an attitude of honor and respect, the bag and its contents are able to bring the shaman in touch with powers of his or her innermost being. Very often, a shaman will carry one or more crystals or other objects that accompanied him or her on the vision quest and will use the stored energy to enhance healing and other ceremonies and sacred rites.

Medicine bags are usually hand stitched and constructed from leather, with beaded adornment. They are small bags, usually hung like necklaces from a cord around the neck, but they can be worn on a belt or carried in a pocket or purse. The exterior designs often act as a protective influence, but the bag itself usually contains additional protection in the form of sacred objects, crystals, feathers, shells, or herbs that have meaning for the shaman, thereby helping him or her to focus intention.

Medicine bags are meant to give guidance, good luck, good health, abundance, and even love to their wearers. They act as a means of personal energetic protection and can be held to help invoke healing and protection. For instance, a shaman consulting with a person in need of balancing may have a medicine bag embroidered or painted with balancing symbols and containing some obsidian stones used for protection. A lay individual who might carry a medicine bag could include a person going to a stressful job interview or other important business meeting. He or she would wear or carry a small medicine bag containing malachite for success and prosperity.

The crystals placed in your bag should represent a part of yourself or your life that you wish to develop or empower. For example, if you want to be more loving, you could place a small piece of rose quartz in your medicine bag.

Medicine bags traditionally contained a clear quartz crystal, a stone that the majority of shamans feel is the most powerful to use. The quartz is usually referred to as "living rock" because it has memory and can be programmed. Shamans around the world have always utilized the special powers of quartz for healing purposes.

The clear quartz crystal is helpful in expanding the mind to open us up to the spiritual world and to help us face our fears and conquer them. Today you can find quartz chips in radios, televisions, computers, and watches, among other things.

Various cultures felt that if one wore the medicine bag close to the body, the sacred power of the bag was stronger and one's personal power was enhanced. In this book,

medicine bags are designed for protection from seen and unseen things and are worn to enhance the wearer's positive attitude and keep negative energy away from the wearer's physical and spiritual self.

Your spiritual or Higher Self is the part of you that knows you better than anyone else—your strengths and your weaknesses, your likes and dislikes, and your past and future, too. It's where your hunches, intuitions, prophetic dreams, and solutions to seemingly unsolvable problems come from. You can think of your Higher Self as the essence of your spirit, the part of you that exists beyond your physical body, beyond space and time. Your Higher Self is connected directly to God/Goddess, All There Is, or, as the Native Americans so beautifully put it, the Great Mystery.

The Healing Crystal Medicine Bag is meant to hold a collection of personal stones that are empowered and meaningful to the wearer. Finding out the power of each crystal that you

> **Medicine bags should be honored and sacred to their caretakers.**

need to carry or wear, based on its type and color, can help to bring harmony into your life and keep it there, and we will provide that information for you.

A person may have several medicine bags, each carried for different reasons. One bag may be for dealing with stress, one for happiness, one for specific healing purposes. The bag itself should be as attractive as possible. It can be decorated with a symbol of your personal deities, signs of protection or health, or a design of your own creation.

The creation of your personal medicine bag is a pure example of "spiritual crafting," as it is a process in which you can nurture your art and soul, find inner peace, and enhance your well-being. To benefit from the spiritual crafting lessons that are in *Healing Crystals*, all you need are a few simple supplies and a desire to connect to a mystical state of grace.

Creating a Healing Crystal Medicine Bag is something anyone can do—and if we listen to the Great Spirit, She will tell us to create medicine bags for others, too, and will guide us regarding what to put in the bags for them; if we know a person who is in need and we pray and ask Her, the Great Spirit will show us. Then we can gift the medicine bag we made to the person.

Your Healing Crystal Medicine Bag can help provide a strong foundation for your spiritual journey. Working with your crystals enables you to heal and transform with ever-increasing ease and clarity. As you carry your Healing Crystal Medicine Bag, it embodies and reflects your intentions and the energies of your spirit and of Mother Earth.

Your Healing Crystals and your personal medicine bags are your special reminders and bonds to your spiritual nature.

# CHAPTER 2

# The Fifteen Master Healing Crystals

*These gems have life in them: their colors speak, say what words fail of.*
—George Elliot

Now that we know beyond a doubt their nature, crystals can help serve as spiritual power tools to teach us how to bring the mind to a greater sense of peace, the body into a more stable, grounded state, and the spirit into connection with the infinite from which springs all creation. Our gemstones can remind us of a higher truth and keep us centered in that light. When we become aware of the qualities of beauty, frequency, and color and their possible uses, stone "medicine" may help us explore what our current needs are and how we may transform certain situations by using a stone as a meditative focus and an inspirational power source. Gems and minerals have patterns and pictures on their surfaces that can transport you to another world, igniting your imagination. They are very tactile and soothing to touch and hold.

The idea of healing with crystals was first popularized in the 1930s when the famous American trance psychic Edgar Cayce claimed that his visions revealed that, in the time of Atlantis, crystals were used as a source of energy. He even described a crystal capstone on a centrally located pyramid that could power airships. He also mentioned various specific stones when prescribing healing protocols for the people he read for.

Each stone becomes a meditative amplifier that can help you to transform your situation. Stones can keep you centered and reminded of a higher truth. By looking to the mineral kingdom for assistance in the healing process, we are connecting to tools that enable us to look deeper within so as to obtain an understanding of the cause of the distress that is creating disease. Distress can be caused by negative beliefs, environmental factors, or difficult interactions with people, any of which can sometimes create havoc in our energy field. When we consume alcohol or drugs, we can also affect our energy fields and cause a disruption in our vibrations.

*IMPORTANT:* Always remember that crystal healing should be used in conjunction with—and not as a substitute for—conventional medicine. There are many factors that make up our well-being. Illnesses need to be tended to by a trusted physician, with yourself as your best advocate. As we all know, however, stress and distress can also have a profound effect on our heath. All thoughts and actions have consequences, creating harmony or disharmony. Disharmony can cause illness. Working with ritual and with healing rocks and crystals can help you to create harmony, handle your stress, and feel better.

Your healing stones offer a beautiful stability and can help you focus on your strengths so that you can use them to compensate for your weaknesses. When we use crystals or stones as healing tools, they have the ability to rebalance a disruptive vibration so that we can be aware of the reason behind the distress.

Below we describe the nature and special healing message of each stone. We have gathered the information for these fifteen Master Healing Crystals through working with them for many years. They are the foundation crystals needed to enhance the power of the medicine bags that you can create using the instructions found in Chapter 7, "Medicine Bag Projects and Patterns," on page 65.

The more you handle and work with the crystals and bags together, the more powerful they will become. Allow them to transform your life. . . .

# Citrine

The citrine's sunny color helps restore the mind in much the same way that basking in the life-giving light of Father Sun does. Citrine helps one to maintain a positive outlook on life. It removes blocks and fears on all levels and helps one to better communicate with others. Citrine helps create a sense of stability, adds energy and emotional balance, and provides a rational approach to things, grounding us in the here and now.

Citrine's energy means that a positive, optimistic attitude will produce a positive outcome. Use it when great self-confidence and self-esteem are needed. Stress and fatigue, either emotional or physical, can make life seem bleak and can make you unable to cope with challenges. Make sure to get enough rest and have some fun. Citrine can help you regain your emotional balance. We all stray from our path. How long it takes us to recover is what determines our successes and failures.

Citrine is one of the best stones for manifesting power on both a practical and a magical level. Because it encourages a healthy ego, self-esteem, and feelings of worth, it empowers its wearer both emotionally and spiritually. New Age healers believe that the stone can increase the significance of dreams and open the mind to new and more positive thought forms. Due to its color, it is believed to strengthen the urinary and endocrine systems.

Citrine is known to clean toxic impurities out of the air and aura. On a supernatural level, it boosts willpower, happiness, and confidence, while reducing self-destructive tendencies. As a result of this, it can also bring good fortune, often in surprising and very unexpected ways.

## Citrine's Message

*Some therapists believe that people who have lost a sense of identity because of an unhappy or abusive relationship can reclaim much of their personal power by meditating with citrine on a regular basis.*

# Agate

Agate is a general protector of the entire body and the entire auric field. Agate can help us to focus on growth and healing. It attracts strength and vitality, and it has the ability to help bring your body into balance. A special property of agate is the blending and balancing of energies for power, protection, and organizational qualities, causing a stabilizing effect. Agate also can help reinforce the body's connection to the Earth. It can give courage and dispel fears, all of which increase self-confidence. It gives you the strength to carry on, even when you feel weak or tired.

Agate offers protection from bad dreams. It also protects one from stress and worry. Agates with banded colors were placed at the head of a sleeper to give rich and varied dreams.

Since our earliest civilizations, agates have been prized gems. They were used in jewelry and as power tools in Babylonia. Conjurers in Persia used the crystal to try to affect the weather. In ancient Asia, agates were used to see the future. Studying the circular patterns helped open the pathway to receive guidance and messages by connecting the conscious and subconscious minds.

Agate can also be enlisted for emotional healing, especially to resolve bitterness and resentments. It is believed to be a stone of harmony and therefore can help soften feelings of envy by grounding agitation. By bringing the elements of one's being into harmony, it can improve relationships. Agate also enhances creativity and stimulates the intellect. Carry an agate when you have to make an important decision.

## Agate's Message

*Placing an agate under your pillow may aid with insomnia and can stimulate pleasant dreams. If you have to deal with numbers, an agate placed on your desk will help you be more precise. You'll also be more analytical as well as creative in your approach to rapidly changing situations.*

# Malachite

Malachite owes its rich green color to the presence of copper, the first metal used by our ancestors for beads and tools. Malachite can help with financial success and with the implementation of new business ideas. To create successful business energy, keep this gemstone in your purse or near your bills. Keep one with you at work, or when you're presenting a project to an important client. Malachite has been used to protect against undesirable business associations.

Malachite may also be used when feelings of lack are blocking your path. If this is true for you, concentrate on the things you have available for your use, not just on the things you own. Copper conducts electricity but it does not own it. Let your past successes empower you. Do not dwell on past disappointments; learn from them. What we do not have are things we fear or do not understand yet. Abundance is an attitude.

Use malachite while you are working through big changes. It will help clear your path and illuminate the steps to your goal.

For protection, malachite can help clear harmful energies. It is a stone that can help create more balance in relationships. This stone reminds us that we have a dual nature; it reflects what is there, negative or positive. That is why malachite has been called the "mirror of the soul."

As a meditative healing stone, malachite can help provide insight into the cause of complaints or confusion. Gazing at the swirling surface of the gemstone can help relax the nervous system, and the calming color can assist in releasing emotions. Keep a piece of malachite in your bedroom to help get rid of nightmares.

## Malachite's Message

*Malachite acts as a mirror, reflecting a person's inner feelings. It can stimulate harmonious expressions of love; bring purification of matters on the material plane; and attract success and good fortune.*

# Rose Quartz

Rose quartz is the stone that can help heal the heart, as it works on an emotional level. It can help you to become more aware of the love that is all around you and can assist you in getting in touch with your emotions. Rose quartz teaches us to love ourselves more, thus opening us up to a greater universal love. When we don't love ourselves fully, we are wounded inside, and a wound will always cry out to be healed. Rose quartz heals emotional wounds by giving compassion and comfort. It can be used to help us to overcome grief.

Rose quartz's properties include inner peace, tranquility, and all matters dealing with giving and receiving affection.

Unlike the hard-edged, pointed crystals of clear quartz, the lovely rose quartz is found in great veins running through Mother Earth like her life's blood. Use it when compassion and generosity need to be shown, or when healing and forgiveness are needed. Rose quartz may help those who have suffered through trauma and the pain of an unhappy childhood. If this is true for you, start by forgiving yourself and others. Be gentle with yourself and others; we have all suffered wounds. From forgiveness can come a path to true healing.

You can also sleep with rose quartz beneath your pillow. The pain of a difficult past problem may come up in dreams, but you can better handle this if you affirm before you go to sleep that you are ready to release the pain.

## Rose Quartz's Message

*Self-fulfillment and inner peace require you to love and nurture yourself and those you care about. Work on how to give love as well as how to receive it. Remember to forgive.*

# Turquoise

One of the most ancient protection stones, turquoise is a sacred stone associated with sky energy because of its color. It also brings sky energy to Earth. Prized in Asian as well as Native American culture, it is known as a multipurpose stone, excellent for promoting a sense of self-awareness and the ability to communicate honestly and from the heart. The stone encourages creative thinking, as many do, but turquoise has the power to help channel that creative energy in a productive and useful way.

Turquoise is considered a lucky stone; it facilitates the attraction of abundance and prosperity. Turquoise has a balancing and grounding influence. Its properties include mental relaxation, stress reduction, confidence, attunement, and physical well-being.

The blue-green turquoise is a stone sacred to many tribes around the world. Use it when you feel the need to call on your spirit guides because you have reached an important time in your life or a crossroads. Turquoise is helpful when you need to restore communication with your Higher Self, and it stimulates your development on the spiritual level. If this is true for you now, it is time to take action to restore your faith. Life often appears meaningless when our faith in the unseen forces that surround and sustain us is weak.

Turquoise can help us not to be distracted by our sorrows. It can help restore our sense of humor so we can enjoy life's gifts as well as its challenges, for we cannot have one without the other. Miracles can be seen every day. Turquoise is a favorite stone among New Age healers, who believe that it has the power to energize the body and spirit, as well as to balance right brain–left brain disparity.

## Turquoise's Message

*True communication is about more than words, and turquoise can help achieve this. Carrying a piece of turquoise will help keep you centered, and wearing it improves all the senses, including the sixth sense.*

# Carnelian

Carnelian grounds energy and helps us to pay attention to the present moment, thus teaching us to focus and manifest our personal power. Use it to encourage strength and the courage to prevail. Carnelian helps to ease stress and anxiety and to improve memory and stimulate sexual impulses.

Use carnelian when barriers of time and space or discouraging news threaten to stop you on your path. If this is true for you now, it is necessary for you to look below the surface of things in order for you to know what is really going on, for things are not what they seem. There is no reason to give up unless and until you know exactly how things stand. Once you do, carnelian can help you regain your courage.

Carry carnelian with you to guard against those who try to use their power over you. It can also help you regain the drive you need to pursue your goals, or help to give birth to a new project or flesh out an existing one. Believed to prevent depression, carnelian helps to build courage by providing self-esteem and an optimistic outlook.

Carnelian got its name because its color is similar to that of meat (as in *carnivorous*). It stimulates energy, physical power, and courage, and helps to ground you on the physical plane.

Early Egyptians used carnelian for amulets, as it was thought to protect the wearer from evil, and to prevent anger and envy. Renaissance sages kept a carnelian amulet in the home to protect themselves from curses.

## Carnelian's Message

*It offers patience while counteracting doubt and negative thoughts. It also assists in decision making by helping us ground ourselves in the present, and make decisions based not on our past, but on our present reality.*

# Lapis

Mother Nature seems to have used the deep blue lapis to capture the sky in solid form. The glittering pyrite inclusions against the deep blue backdrop of this splendid stone create a striking likeness of a galaxy. Lapis is an excellent stone to help with peaceful sleep and psychic dreaming. It can bring matters more clearly to the mind. The stone will allow for cosmic communication with other dimensions of reality. Sleeping with this gemstone can help you see the meaning in your dreams more clearly by allowing you to interpret and understand the messages or information that your subconscious is providing.

Use lapis to help with success in business and other worldly pursuits. It is good to use for humanitarian quests and interests, as it has far-reaching effects, just like a galaxy. Early cultures valued lapis lazuli more highly than gold. In Egypt it was customary to bury a lapis lazuli scarab with the dead, as it was believed to offer protection. It is also believed to enhance higher love, powers of intelligence, and concentrated intention.

Lapis can help you focus on universal brotherhood and sisterhood cooperation to produce abundance. Some other properties of lapis are illumination, wisdom, mental insight, and clarity of thought. It may also help when systems of information exchange, transportation, and communication are blocked. Lapis can help you to communicate your deeply felt beliefs and put them into practice in the outer world. It can help shy, introverted people express themselves. Expressing your true self can free energies you would otherwise waste repressing. Lapis helps to release old, buried emotions, thereby helping to dispel depression.

## Lapis Lazuli's Message

*Meditate with lapis when you need all methods for moving people, services, and facts to be as direct and simple as possible. Use it when you need a higher perspective on your situation. When blocked channels are cleared by lapis, expect energies to be a bit chaotic initially, before they calm down.*

# Opal

The opal owes its fiery beauty to the refractions of tiny imperfections and water trapped within its crystalline cells. The dance of color in opal is the result of light being radiated by microscopic silica spheres. Watching the colors flash when luminous sparkles flicker within an opal gemstone leaves you with little doubt that this is a beautiful and powerful crystal.

An opal may bring you enlightenment, integrity, or even the fires of romance. It enhances the emotions and amplifies personal traits. Opal can assist you with almost any aspect of your life, such as joy, love, or success. Let your opal fire up your heart's desire and make your wishes come true. Opal helps magnetize opportunities for things to happen in exciting new ways. Use opal to call in good luck and good fortune, to initiate in yourself what light workers call prosperity consciousness—a feeling that you have all that you need to get what you want—and to encourage new ideas.

Opal acts as a magnet by helping to illuminate your interests and ability to see great possibilities. It encourages you to dance your life by amplifying your emotions and heightening your experiences.

There are two main opal categories, common and precious. Precious opals are those with the famous rainbow sparkles. Common opals are stones without fire.

If you are bored or in a rut, either type of opal can spark a flame of passion and ignite your imagination, helping you see solutions to mundane problems. It turns up the power in everything.

Adding this gemstone to any prayer, ritual, or creative work will strengthen your intention and affirmation. Shamans used opals in important ceremonies such as vision quests. For divination and oracle use, you may want to wear or hold an opal. It will enhance your attunement to the messages of the Tarot or other psychic readings.

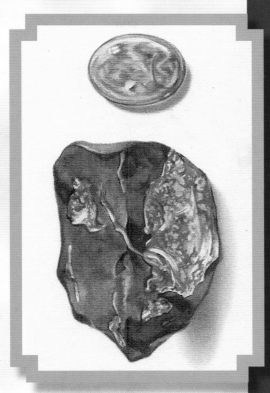

## Opal's Message

*It magnifies your thoughts and feelings and promotes all intuitive abilities. In ancient times the opal was thought to be a very powerful healing stone and was believed to open up the senses of the third eye. The opal can be a doorway to your spiritual awareness.*

# Amethyst

The amethyst's purple color, the color of pure spirit and the seemingly magical things connected with it, is rare in nature. Use it when you need approval from the universe, or when peace and calm are needed. If this is so, try this basic meditation: Take a few moments to breathe calmly and focus your attention on your breathing. Let all thoughts drift away like clouds. After a while you may sense the small voice of your Higher Self. Be aware of the natural fear of not being in control or not knowing exactly what to do next on your path. Amethyst can help you trust in yourself and "let go and let God/Goddess." Holding an amethyst may help ease the pain and sorrow of a loss or defeat.

Easily recognizable for its beautiful color, this stone is known to promote personal serenity and feelings of peace. Amethyst derives its reputation for being a healing stone from ancient and medieval times when it was used as an amulet against drunkenness. The amethyst is a power stone on many levels; it holds the intention to heal the body as well as the spirit. The amethyst has long been used to open one's psychic centers.

In folklore, this stone is believed to have a soothing and relaxing effect. Holistic healers sometimes use amethyst to ease toothache and bruising. It calms an overactive mind and brings a sense of tranquility to those who are frazzled by overwork. It is used as a dream stone and to help insomnia. For those who are psychically sensitive, it can improve the ability of second sight. As an amulet, it can be worn as a protective talisman against jealousy, envy, and deception.

## Amethyst's Message

*Amethyst is believed to be helpful in the treatment of insomnia. By putting an amethyst under the pillow, the troubled sleeper should experience better REM sleep, with less chance of fitful slumber.*

# Clear Quartz

Clear quartz, also known as rock crystal or quartz crystal, has been held sacred by many cultures because of its hard-edged clarity. It is used for meditation, transformation, stability, knowledge, protection, healing, and enlightenment. Use it when you desire clarity on an issue or need an answer to be crystal clear.

The most renowned use for quartz has always been the crystal ball. Quartz crystal possesses qualities stimulating to clairvoyance and helps you fall asleep when you want to. It is the choice material for divination. It has the effect of enabling the mind to project itself and become one with everything, which is why it is useful for crystal gazing. To use it, clear your mind of all worries and anxiety. You do not need to know the future now, only that you will be able to handle whatever comes. Worry accomplishes nothing but distracts you and prevents you from living fully in the moment, the ultimate gift of the Great Spirit.

Quartz crystals have always been used in many spiritual traditions. Some Native American tribes and the Aborigines incorporated the crystals in ceremonies and religious rites to call upon healing and protection. Use it after a toxic incident when there is a need for purification. Keep a piece of clear quartz in your sacred space.

Use this stone for shielding out harmful energies or for absorbing energies that you desire to release. If this is what you wish to do, you must be clear that the only way to purify the situation is to act immediately to completely remove the impurity and everything connected with it; otherwise, its hold will only become stronger. Always remember to clean and clear all of your crystals after working with them.

## Quartz Crystal's Message

It is a receiver, amplifier, conductor, and generator of energy. As a universal conduit, it amplifies, focuses, stores, and clears energies. Its properties remind us that deep within each person is a clear crystal essence of spirit waiting to be revealed.

# Obsidian

Obsidian is a stone of protection that prevents one from becoming emotionally drained by others. It can work as a shield against unwanted vibrations and help protect you from physical or emotional harm. Native Americans traditionally kept this stone on them to protect them from negative energies or psychic attack.

Obsidian tends to give emotional stability in times of high stress, in part by preventing the draining of energy from the body. The energy to help with grounding is the strongest attribute available in this stone. Keeping obsidian with you helps prevent negative thought patterns and can also be used for space clearing by removing the vibrations of unhelpful or distracting entities.

Obsidian is an excellent crystal-gazing tool. Some practitioners have better luck peering into obsidian's black depths to reach their subconscious messages than into a traditional clear quartz crystal ball.

The black, glasslike obsidian is forged in the fires of volcanoes, Mother Earth's way of clearing away the old to make way for the new. It helps with transitions, so use it when you realize that the old must be completely released before the new can enter your life. It may also be useful when obsessions and negative thoughts and actions are blocking you. If this is happening to you, try to let every negative thought and action you encounter in yourself or in others remind you to think and act positively.

This gemstone may help you recover forgotten abilities within yourself. Obsidian can help you to become more aware of your true place in the universe by sharpening your inner vision. It will also help you become more aware of your imperfections and at the same time provide constructive solutions and insights.

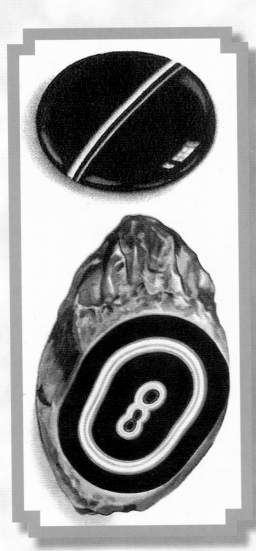

## Obsidian's Message

*Do not give in to the
desire to think and act
negatively, even if others
do. This is a difficult but
most powerful teaching.
Our negativity comes
back to us in unpleasant
ways. Obsidian may help
you cope with negativity
and keep centered in
unstable times. Do
not resist change.*

# Garnet

The garnet takes its name from the resemblance of its deep red color to that of the pomegranate. It can help bring success in things you passionately believe in and, if appropriate, the sparks of passion or even sexual energy between you and another of your choosing. It may also be useful when wisdom and balance in this most important exchange of energies are needed. If this is so, look within to see if true love, tenderness, and genuine respect and caring are part of your romantic passion.

Garnet can help bring balance and self-awareness and destroy flightiness, leaving in its place love, romance, and sometimes lustiness, for those who need it.

Because of its rich color and association with the root chakra (see Chapter 12), the garnet suggests a powerful influence for sensuality and sexuality. It may help put you in touch with your animal instincts, enabling you to act and react with their pure body wisdom. Therapists who believe in the power of gemstones use the garnet in counseling couples whose sexual chemistry has begun to wane.

For meditation and ritual purposes, the garnet is used primarily as a power stone, to enhance self-confidence and help to manifest personal and career goals. Garnet has properties useful for giving inspiration during times of confusion. The red garnet is a stone of profound love and helps to ensure fidelity in relationships. It is a stone of patience and persistence and is also emblematic of spiritual awareness and compassion.

Garnet is highly versatile…it encourages the wearer to search for answers—and the answers that come as a result of this search will be helpful and important ones. Worn on a regular basis, the stone is believed to boost energy and stimulate romantic love.

## Garnet's Message

*Because it has a bold energy, the garnet makes a perfect amulet for someone whose confidence or self-esteem needs bolstering. Because of its warm vibrations, it makes a good meditation stone for security and intimacy.*

# Hematite

Hematite helps to dissolve negative energy and works as a shield of armor for any person or thing. Hematite can be worn to focus energy patterns and emotions, for better balance among the mental, physical, and spiritual. Hematite is good for increasing intuition. It has special electric and magnetic qualities, enhancing your ability to receive channeled information.

Hematite can help create calmness and peace, allowing you to be more centered and able to have realistic expectations. It will aid you in reaching for your dreams while staying grounded in the practical world. It can help you to become aware of your connection to Mother Earth.

Hematite's use as a healing stone goes back to ancient Egypt and Mesopotamia. It has been found adorning artifacts and jewelry in the tombs of the pharaohs. The name comes from the Greek word for blood. Native American folklore states that war paint made from hematite makes the warrior invincible in battle.

Use this gem to transform harmful energies into loving ones and to nurture your own inner peace, happiness, and self-control. Hematite works to make it easier for you to love others. It stimulates your aspirations regardless of what you perceive as possible or impossible, releasing all judgment.

Hematite is an excellent stone to keep on your desk to refresh your aura and counter the ill effects of electromagnetic conditions from your computer. It assists in grounding your anxieties while adding a healthy level of spiritual energy to your everyday reality. It can be used to create calm, dispel fear, and induce tranquil sleep. It pushes out old emotional wounds and brings in renewed love and joy.

## Hematite's Message

*As a power stone, hematite is good for mental dexterity, for simplifying and solving complex problems, and for improving technical skills. If you need to improve or understand a personal relationship, carry a piece of hematite.*

# Amber

Amber is the oldest geological specimen to be used in jewelry. Archeologists digging primitive sites near the Baltic Sea have found evidence of amber jewelry that is approximately forty thousand years old.

This good-luck stone brings the purifying, revitalizing force of the Sun and the absorptive, transmuting energy of the Earth together to create a powerful tool. In mythology, Apollo cried amber tears after being banished from Olympus. Medieval housewives would burn amber to bring good energy into their homes. Native American tribal healers used it in fire ceremonies.

Ancient Greeks discovered that if they rubbed a piece of amber vigorously, it became electrically charged. The early name for amber was *electron*, which is the root word for today's electricity. Amber's use as a power tool reaches back to man's earliest history.

Amber absorbs negative energy, helps to ground one to the Earth plane, and protects the sensitive person. It helps to distribute vitality to our aura, and it centers a person during meditation. Amber can be worn or carried to help calm the nerves. Amber allows a person to receive from the universe, yet assists one in remaining physically alert.

Amber is not technically a crystal but is an organic compound. Some 360 million years ago, extinct pine trees oozed thick, sticky resins. As these resins flowed, a variety of living and decomposing matter became trapped inside. Then the resin was made to fossilize under the great pressure from the Earth's changes. Many ancient traditions associate amber with the universal life force because, essentially, actual life has been trapped inside.

## Amber's Message

*Amber is excellent at removing self-imposed obstacles on any projects you are attempting to create. It enhances a constructive way of behaving, fueled by self-confidence. It can attract new friendships and aid in focusing your intentions for manifestation, helping you to reach your goals.*

# Jade

This stone acts in a protective way, on both the physical and spiritual levels. Jade has long been believed to facilitate and fortify a long life. The Chinese have traditionally held jade in very high esteem, and it has a lovely history as a protective talisman.

Amulets of animals were carved to promote a healthier, longer life and would attract the protection of the spirits when needed. Jade was also used in rituals to attract wealth and fortune. Statues of this stone for abundance and protection were common. Dishes were often carved from jade. The gem was also believed to symbolize longevity, and therefore food or drink contained in jade vessels would absorb that energy.

Jade energy bestows peace, calmness, harmony, tranquility, and mental clarity, and encourages one to safely express one's true feelings and emotions. It strongly influences the matters of the heart and can help to improve relationships. Jade is wonderful for repairing relationship connections and ties that have been lost or broken.

This stone also promotes a more unified environment so you may accomplish compromise with partners, family members, or co-workers. Jade inspires and promotes creative thought.

For business matters, you can use jade to unite diverse individuals and get them working toward common goals. It aids in creating a harmonious atmosphere and a desire for success and abundance without materialism or greed.

Jade is also favorable for strengthening clear reasoning and in so doing stimulates excellent decision making. Because it has a balancing effect, jade motivates the wearer to believe that his or her plans and ambitions are worthy of success.

## Jade's Message

*This is a helpful stone for those who have a nervous temperament or who are easily overwhelmed. The loving energies of this stone will assist you in recovering from emotional trauma because it provides grounding energy and a sense of security.*

# CHAPTER 3

# How to Choose Your Healing Crystals and Stones

*When we become aware of its qualities of radiant beauty, frequency, and possible uses, stone "medicine" may help us explore what our current needs are and how we may transform certain situations by using a stone as a meditative focus and an inspirational power source.*

You can choose rocks, gemstones, or crystals for their color, shape, and exquisiteness or for emotions or associations triggered inside of you when you look at them. It is important to honor the stones you select as the "ancient ones" containing the cosmic pulsations of timeless wisdom. Every stone has its own particular type of vibration. That vibration may affect our minds, bodies, and spirits, as well as our environment. The key to choosing crystals and stones is to use your intuition. You may feel a shiver or an "aha" moment when you hold the crystal that is right for you. Remember, a stone that wants to be with you will resonate with you. Some gemstones have qualities that seem to match your personality characteristics.

Another approach is to choose stones according to the qualities you want to develop in yourself. For example, if you have a hard time with money issues, you might choose malachite. If you need to make an important decision, ground yourself with hematite.

Whether shopping for crystals in a store or online, take a quiet moment to ask your Higher Self, "Is this crystal, gem, or stone the right one for my highest good and greatest joy?" If your intuition says "Yes!" then proceed with your purchase. If you get a "No!" then keep looking. Your sixth sense speaks softly and is as much a feeling as a word. Yet it is the best guide to determine which will be your own personal healing crystals.

Most people will choose the crystal that will best assist them in the situation they need it for. Crystals are often used for clearing the mind, for helping with a physical problem, for meditation, for charms of protection for yourself or your home, for healing, for chakra work, for altars and rituals, or for anything that seems suitable.

A good healing stone should fit comfortably into the palm of your hand. You may feel that the crystal you pick is highly sensitive, aware of your needs, and ready to help. The stones we suggest in this book are very affordable and easy to find.

Select the crystal that has the properties to help you with a specific issue. The following list has been provided in order to help you with your choice, or simply feel which stones you are drawn to....

# CHAPTER 4

# Which Stone Are You Drawn To?

## Citrine

The citrine may attract you when greater self-confidence and self-esteem are needed. If this is true now, heal your relationship with your father or other authority figures. Make sure to get enough rest and have some fun. If you have lots of ideas but can't seem to materialize them, then citrine may give you the security and power you need to feel you deserve to manifest your ideas.

## Agate

Agate may attract you if you are drawn to connect to nature and nature spirits. If you want to understand yourself better, then agate can help you to understand the self while strengthening self-esteem. Also, if you feel sad, agate will help you get through and look to tomorrow as a better, brighter day. You may need the strength of agate to carry on.

## Malachite

Malachite may attract you when success with money and investments is near. Let your past successes empower you. Do not dwell on past disappointments; just learn from them. What we do not have are things we fear or do not understand yet. If you have low self-esteem and feel you don't deserve success or abundance, then malachite can help boost and balance an inadequate sense of self.

## Rose Quartz

Rose quartz may attract you when compassion and generosity need to be shown. It may also appear when healing and forgiveness are needed. If this is so, start by forgiving yourself and others. From forgiveness can come a path for healing. If you are intolerant of others, then rose quartz addresses the intolerance we feel toward those people who mirror what we view as our own faults.

## Turquoise

Turquoise may attract you when you are neglecting your development on the spiritual level. It is time to take action to restore your faith. Miracles can be seen every day. Turquoise can help you not to be too distracted by past sorrows. If you have lots of ideas but it is difficult for you to express them, turquoise helps you to clarify ideas—and to access the help of others to realize them.

## Carnelian

Carnelian may attract you when it is necessary for you to look below the surface of things in order to know what is really going on. You may soon be giving birth to a new project or fleshing out an existing one. If you have a hard time making decisions or need to focus, carnelian helps you to be grounded in the present and to realize your current needs.

## Lapis

Lapis may attract you when success in business and other worldly pursuits is near. Keep all information as direct and simple as possible. Lapis can help you build the cooperation that produces wealth. If you would like to be more successful with your ideas, choose lapis for feeling confident about using your unique inventiveness.

## Opal

Opal may attract you when a time of luck and good fortune is near. If you refrain from criticizing unless you have a plan to improve the situation, you may enjoy new degrees of pleasure and romance. Ruffled feathers can be smoothed. If you wish you could express yourself more artistically, then choose opal for its ability to help balance the logical, practical, and intuitive or visionary sides of the brain.

## Amethyst

Amethyst may attract you when seemingly magical things are about to happen, when a deep and soulful experience is present. Take a few moments to breathe calmly and focus your attention on your breathing. Let all thoughts drift away like clouds. If you would like more serenity in your life, then amethyst is the most recommended stone for stress relief.

## Clear Quartz

Clear quartz may attract you when there is a need for clarity and purity. Clear your mind of all worries and anxiety. Live fully in the moment. If you have goals but find it difficult to get from where you are to where you want to be, then clear quartz has the most focused energy and is the most powerful crystal to program for goals.

## Obsidian

Obsidian may attract you when it is time to clear away the old to make way for the new. If negative thoughts and actions are blocking you, try to let each one you encounter remind you to think and act positively. If you wish you could know what's preventing you from having what you want, then obsidian helps to bring the hidden to the surface. Be sure you want to know!

## Garnet

Garnet is a stone of purity and truth; it may attract you when there is about to be success from what you believe in passionately. It can also mean that sparks of sexual energy may soon fly. The garnet is a symbol of love and compassion. It may also put you in touch with your animal instincts, enabling you to feel secure and act with their pure body wisdom.

## Hematite

Hematite may attract you when you need to be more organized. It aids logical thinking and planning. If you calm your mind, it will also improve your memory. Hematite brings practical insights and decisions. Hematite helps to deflect negativity. If you find that you pick up on other people's moods, then hematite can help you to deflect, rather than absorb, the moods of others.

## Amber

Amber will attract you when you need to calm your anxiety. It helps to keep you centered and increases knowledge, wisdom, and enlightenment. Try not to absorb negative energy from others. Amber has a powerful connection to the Earth, and therefore it is a great grounding tool. If you are feeling stressed, amber helps with any kind of emotional turmoil.

## Jade

Jade may attract you when you need a peaceful healing of your emotions. It has a calming effect, enhancing the meditative state and creating pure thoughts, spiritual insight, and nurturing. Wearing jade helps to control the temperament and gives strength during periods of great activity.

# How to Clear and Program Your Crystals

## Simple Grounding Exercises

At the beginning of this book we grounded your understanding of crystal energy, taking you from the most basic meaning of what constitutes a crystal all the way to an understanding of why their ability to focus and regulate the vibrational frequency of atoms, ions, X-rays, electricity, and light enables them to be used to focus and regulate the energies of our being. It is now time to learn the shamanic technique of grounding yourself prior to doing healing work.

Grounding returns you to your connection to Mother Earth. Too much energy input, whether it is environmental or emotional, can cause you to separate from your body. You might experience a feeling of disorientation, confusion, and separation. Here are a couple of quick and effective exercises to ground yourself. You will notice how much more centered you feel after you perform them.

# Earth Connection

Stand in an area large enough to extend your arms out from your sides without touching anything. With your arms by your sides, take a deep breath and raise your arms into a horizontal position at the shoulder, palms down. As you breathe in, imagine you are drawing in the Earth energies through your palms; feel a tingling sensation. Hold your arm position and your breath for a moment, and then release your breath with a strong and loud *hah* sound. While pushing your palms down toward the ground, imagine you are blasting your energy into the Earth. Make the sound again. Do this three times.

# Tree Connection

Sit in a comfortable position. Imagine that you are a tree. Send roots down through your feet to the center of the Earth. Attach your roots deep in the Earth, and draw its vibrant growing energy up through your roots, feet, lower body, middle body, upper chest, arms, shoulders, neck, and the top of your head as a spray of light and color radiating through and out of you like branches of light energy. Continue to draw the light energy up through your tree-body and around and down again in a circle of vitality. After three times, open your eyes.

The clearer the energy of a healing stone, the more powerful it is. A cleared crystal feels positive and bright. A crystal that needs clearing may feel lifeless or dull. Crystals and healing gemstones need to be cleared as soon as they are purchased, and after intense use. Remember that they can get "tired" from overuse. They are prone to depletion (like us), so take good care of them. Clearing should be done before using any stone you are drawn to. Here are a number of ways to effectively clear and clean your Healing Crystals:

# Water

When using water to cleanse crystals, hold your crystal in the water source of your choice. The length of time needed for cleansing is up to you. When the crystal feels clean, and you can feel the energy flowing, it is cleared and ready for your healing session. Very porous stones should not be cleaned with water.

# Sound

To clear your crystals with sound, use a bell, a tuning fork, or anything else that creates a pure sound. You can also chant the *om* meditation sound into it. Hold your stone close to the origin of the sound until you feel the energy in the crystal become clear.

## Breath

The breath method uses your breath to "blow away" any negativity from the stone. Simply hold the stone in your hand and blow on it. While blowing, ask the universe to clear and refresh the crystal, helping it to release stale, old, or stagnant energy.

## Smudging

A quick way to cleanse your healing stones is to smudge them with burning cedar or sage. Simply hold the burning sage or cedar stick while passing your stone through the smoke. Be sure to work safely with the matches and the fire, and extinguish the flame properly.

## Burying

Your crystal can be buried in a bowl of dried herbs such as rosemary, sage, cedar, or sandalwood, or in a bowl of rose petals. Crystals may also be buried in the Earth. Indoors or out, dig a shallow hole the size of your crystal in the Earth. Then place your crystal in the hole and cover with it soil. Be sure to place a marker of some sort to allow you to find your stone again.

## Salt

For this method, you will need sea salt and a container to hold the salt and the crystal. Be careful with your crystals in the salt because some of your stones are delicate.

## Moonlight

Moonlight is another way of clearing your gemstones. Simply place your crystals outside in a safe place where the moonlight can shine on them. Use your intuition to feel how long the stones need to be out.

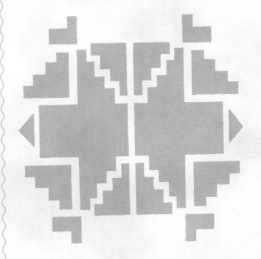

# How to Program a Crystal

Crystals can receive and hold your intention, and this is called programming. Information and intention are energy thought forms: visions, wishes, hopes, and affirmations that are powered by practice and belief.

First, have a clear intention such as feeling peaceful, creating abundance, or attracting more love into your life. Focus on the purpose of your wish and the end result you would like to have. Place the crystal against your brow, between your eyes—this is where your powerful and intuitive third eye is located. Close your eyes and go inside the crystal to create a personal thought form. Visualize the end result in your third eye. See it, say it, and feel it to make it real. See the colors, hear the sounds, and experience the emotions of your wish. When it feels real, breathe the vision into your crystal; then open your eyes. The vision vibration will be stored in the crystal until it is purposefully cleared out with the clearing techniques, below.

**Step 1**   Clear your crystal with whatever method you prefer (see page 60), and then sit down with your crystal in a quiet place and get comfortable.

**Step 2**   Hold the crystal in your dominant hand (right hand if right handed) and clear your mind of anxious thoughts. Breathe deeply and slowly. Start to focus on your intention for the programming of your crystal.

**Step 3**   Focus by repeating a mantra of descriptive words aloud. For instance, if you want to program your crystal to bring focus for an important project, repeat the words "I need more focus for this project" over and over again. A whisper is fine, or you can repeat your mantra in your mind's eye.

**Step 4**   Repeat your intention as you place your other hand over your crystal to lock the vibrations into the crystal.

**Step 5**   Continue to repeat your intention while holding the crystal cupped in both hands and until it feels as though the crystal has accepted the programming fully.

**Step 6**   Open your hands and thank the crystal. To access the programming, simply hold and rub the crystal and ask for its programming to be released whenever you need it, or until you clear the crystal for your next intention.

# CHAPTER 6
# Creating a Healing Crystal Medicine Bag:
## The Way of Spiritual Crafting

*All the means of action—*

*the shapeless masses—*

*the materials—lie*

*everywhere about us.*

*What we need is the*

*celestial fire to change the*

*flint into the transparent*

*crystal bright and clear.*

*That fire is genius.*

—Henry Wadsworth Longfellow

I, Amy, am an artist, and I have always worked with fabrics, trims, and embellishments.

As a child I lived in the country. I was encouraged to be in touch with nature and, as a result, I became a gatherer of magical bits and pieces of rocks, shells, and dried flowers, which I would incorporate or sew into my early artworks. Since I was little, I was encouraged to be in touch with my mystical side. I loved to make dish gardens. I would get a big dish and go through the woods and get different little stones, mosses, mushrooms, and a plant called jack-in-the-pulpit; my favorite part was getting the mirror to look like a little pool. These rock gardens were forerunners of my collaged landscapes. Even now, each time I create a piece of art, I sing into it, or "enchant" it, to help further empower its healing gifts.

I remember visiting the American Museum of Natural History in New York City when I was very young, and coming home with boxes of mineral specimens, which I pored over for hours and treasured. These were my secret possessions. Every stone had a story to tell me. Collecting gems and stones became a lifelong pursuit. My mother, Jessie Spicer Zerner, was also an artist and a "stone hunter," and when I was growing up in

Pennsylvania, we spent many days searching for fossils and rocks along the Loyalsock Creek, and found exciting keepsakes that have always been proudly displayed, a reminder of a shared passion.

Monte and I now bring back stones and precious gems from our many trips, each of which provides us with happy memories of where they came from and with associations about what they symbolize. Every room of our home is adorned with marvelous and rare crystals, and we love to gaze at them, as well as use them in our spiritual practice. One of our favorite trips was to Herkimer, New York, where we actually dug and mined for Herkimer crystals. It was an amazing experience, and we cherish those sacred gems.

We performed a special ritual when we built my large, two-story art studio in 1987. We consecrated it as a temple using ancient techniques. Monte marched around the cinderblock foundation seven times forward and seven times backward. We wrote our favorite sayings on the walls with heavy felt markers, like metaphysical graffiti artists, and though the carpenters thought us a bit strange, I think they liked it. Before the large wooden beams for the floor arrived, we put healing crystals and jewels in the holes of the

cinderblocks, each placement accompanied by a different temple-blessing prayer from a different culture. We wanted my studio to be a consecrated temple to the Goddess.

I love working in my studio—it is truly a sacred space, and I have happily made many fabric collage tapestries there. I have also been a fashion designer for many years, and I create couture jackets and ensembles for many notable women, including Elizabeth Taylor, Patti LaBelle, Shirley MacLaine, Oprah Winfrey, Louise Hay, and Martha Stewart. I sell my very high-end fashions at Bergdorf Goodman in New York City, the finest store in the world.

The scraps of fabrics and trims all around me in my studio moved me to begin making medicine bags for my crystals. I now think of this process as "spiritual crafting," as it is important and natural for me to incorporate my spiritual beliefs into my artwork. This attention and respect makes the medicine bags and healing crystals happy. The medicine bags I make are intended to keep cherished crystals safe and sound. Each bag is one of a kind. I am pleased to share my designs with you in these pages.

Your personal medicine bag should reflect your own unique qualities and tastes. Hopefully, it should help to empower your goals and aspirations. A Healing Crystal Medicine Bag made with your own hands and vision contains your love more than any commercially made item ever could. Creating a medicine bag reinforces a desired goal or experience.

Before you begin, clear your mind and connect to your creative source by saying a short prayer. Next, choose the intention that you want to reflect upon. I recommend choosing one attribute, such as prosperity or confidence or clarity. It also is very important, as you make and sew your bag, to say any prayers that come to your mind for assistance, guidance, and protection.

Be sure to gather a range of favorite fabrics, trims, feathers, shells, coins, charms, ideas, and materials to draw from when working on your medicine bag. It is a very enjoyable activity to go out and search for good materials. I have been collecting for many years and so have many boxes full of "sacred stuff" that I have found in thrift shops and flea markets and that have been gifted to me by friends who know and love what I do.

As you sort through your materials to make your selections, repeat the intention word in your mind, and you will be guided to select appropriately. Set aside anything that you feel complements your theme: a certain color of fabric, a perfect ribbon, a silver bead.

You will want to choose fabrics and beads in your favorite colors, as well as materials and textures that give you pleasant sensory experiences, such as smooth satin fabric or ribbon or an antique embroidered appliqué. If you prefer not to use real leather, use microsuede cloth or pleather, a synthetic leather fabric.

There is no end to the wonderful array of textiles and materials to choose from. For example, you may want to use feathers. Feathers sometimes appear and come to us unexpectedly, bringing messages from loved ones, angels, spirits, and spirit guides. Some believe these ephemeral messengers carry our prayers over to the spirit realm when used in ritual and prayer.

Be inspired to use any special embellishments that have a particular attraction, symbolism, and meaning for you. It is fun to treasure hunt!

Feel free to decorate your medicine bag in any way you choose. Use your fabric paints and markers to paint images on it that are meaningful. The images should reflect the purpose of the medicine bag. You may like to incorporate animals or Celtic symbols or astrological signs, depending on for what and whom the bag is intended. This is all completely up to you.

You can use a sewing machine if you have one available, but all of the following patterns can be sewn by hand. While you sew, think about the purpose of the particular bag you are creating. That energy and spirit will go into your bag, too, along with your healing crystals. The act of sewing is threading the pure essence of you, the creator, and your intention into the bag, giving it a stronger power.

We also have provided a section at the end of the book with lists of suppliers for all the materials necessary to create your bags, as well as sources for purchasing your crystals.

When the bag you make is finished, you will add your specially chosen crystals.

I have designed twelve medicine bag patterns and ideas to work with, but feel free to experiment and to make them for different purposes and for gifts. Use the examples and patterns as guides to inspire your imagination and ignite your connection to your shamanic path.

# CHAPTER 7

# Medicine Bag Projects and Patterns

IMPORTANT: We are providing you with patterns for twelve medicine bags. Space considerations, however, require us to print some of the patterns smaller on the page than for their intended use. To size them properly, please enlarge them on a copy machine by the indicated percentage. Then trace the pattern onto your selected material. Patterns without enlargement percentages indicated are already at 100%.

# Vision Quest Medicine Bag

*Your vision quest is an effort to return to the feeling of wholeness by turning inward for power. The search for this inner power is the "medicine" the shamans seek. They want that which will heal them and make them whole.*

## You Will Need

- 12" x 12" square of microsuede cloth, soft leather, or suede for body of bag
- Material for template
- Sharp scissors and/or leather shears
- 10" length of beaded or fringed trim for bag front
- Pins
- 10" length of ribbon for top edge of bag front
- 2" x 2" square of ribbon or fabric for bag-front appliqué
- Strong, sharp needle (e.g., glove and leather needle)
- Heavyweight thread (e.g., carpet and button thread)
- Charms and/or other embellishments for bag front
- 18" length of ⅜" cording for bag edges
- 1 yard of braid or cord for strap

After you create your medicine bag, it needs to be empowered and filled with your crystals. Place the bag and all the cleaned and cleared crystals you wish to put inside it on a table. We like to light candles and play soft music in the background. Relax and hold each crystal in your hand, close your eyes, and think about what you would like it to do, about your hopes and wishes.

# Assembly

## Step 1

Use the pattern on page 70 to make a template. Use the template to cut two pieces from the microsuede cloth, soft leather, or suede. You will use one piece for the front of the bag and one for the back of the bag.

## Step 2

Pin the beaded trim along the top edge of the right side of the bag front. Trim to fit. Machine or hand stitch in place, leaving space to place a ribbon border above it. Pin and stitch the 10" length of ribbon in place. Trim to fit.

## Step 3

Stitch the 2" square of ribbon or fabric to the center of the bag front.

## Step 4

With a strong, sharp needle and heavyweight thread, hand stitch the charms or other embellishments to the 2" square of ribbon or fabric.

## Step 5

Starting at the top corner of the bag front, and with right sides together, align the raw edge of the ⅜" cording with the raw edge of the bag. Stitch the cording to the bag around the side and bottom edges using a ¼" seam allowance. Don't pin the piping; just ease it gently around the curves as you sew. Trim to fit.

## Step 6

Place the bag front and back right sides together and machine stitch around the side and bottom edges, using a ⅝" seam allowance. Leave the top edge of the bag open.

## Step 7

Turn the bag right side out and machine or hand stitch the ends of the braid or cording to the top corners of the bag to make the strap.

PATTERN: Vision Quest Medicine Bag

Enlarge 134%

⅝" seam allowance

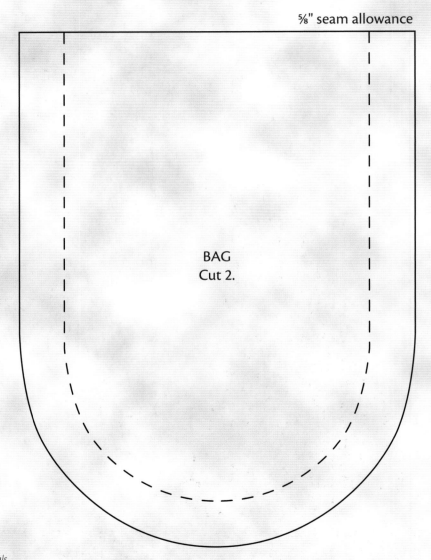

BAG
Cut 2.

# Pathfinder Medicine Bag

*Healing Crystals*

*Oh, Mother Earth, mother of us all, I release my fears, doubts, and negativity into the fire in your heart center. I feel your love and protection.*

*I thank you for protecting me and surrounding me with your pure love and light.*

## You Will Need

- 12" x 12" square of microsuede cloth, soft leather, or suede for body of bag

- Material for template

- Sharp scissors and/or leather shears

- Beaded embellishment, gemstone, or cabochon for bag front

- Strong, sharp needle (e.g., glove and leather needle)

- Waxed cotton thread or linen cord

- Leather hole punch

- 1 yard of leather lace for drawstring

- Jewelry or leather cement (optional)

- Beads for drawstring (optional); make sure beads have large enough holes to accommodate the leather lace

## Assembly

### Step 1

Use the pattern on page 75 to make a template. Use the template to cut two pieces from the microsuede cloth, soft leather, or suede. You will use one piece for the front of the bag and one for the back of the bag.

A shaman's tasks include:

• Restoring wellness

• Purifying energy

• Mending discord

• Improving relationships

• Interpreting visions

• Giving meaning to events

### Step 2

Attach the beaded embellishment, gemstone, or cabochon to the bag front either by hand with a strong, sharp needle and waxed cotton thread or linen cord, or with jewelry or leather cement.

### Step 3

Place the wrong sides of the bag front and back pieces together. Use the needle and waxed cotton thread or linen cord to hand stitch the pieces together, ¼" from the raw edges along the sides, and as indicated by the pattern for the bag bottom. Leave the top edge of the bag open.

### Step 4

Again using the pattern as a guide, cut fringe in the bottom edge of the bag, below the bottom seam, with sharp scissors or leather shears. Take care not to cut into the seam.

### Step 5

Using a leather hole punch, carefully make eight evenly spaced holes around the top edge of the bag for the drawstring.

### Step 6

Thread the lace through the holes, finishing with a knot in the center front. Add beads to the drawstring if desired.

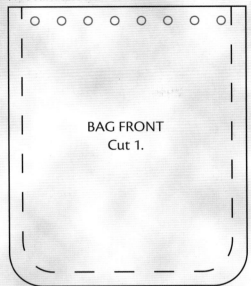

**BAG FRONT**
Cut 1.

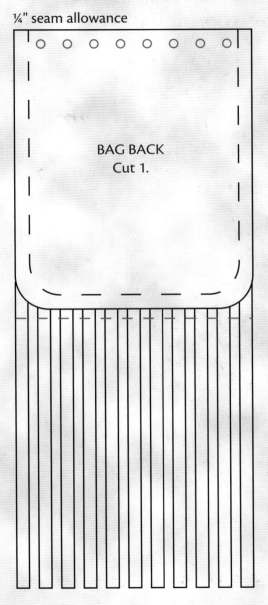

**BAG BACK**
Cut 1.

PATTERN: **Pathfinder Medicine Bag**

Enlarge 142%

# Animal Power Medicine Bag

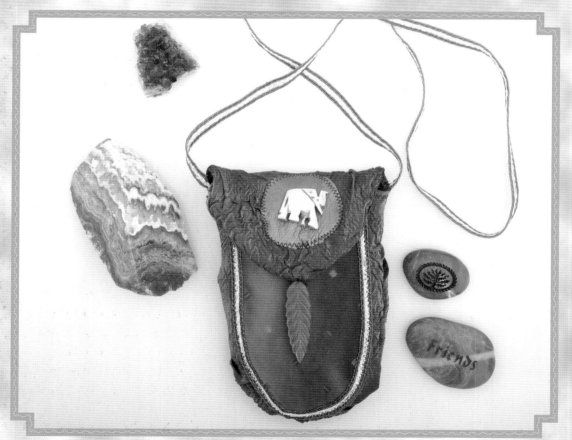

*Animals are our sisters and brothers, our friends and neighbors, and they can be our teachers if only we will listen to the lessons they teach us by their very being. The Wheel of Life tells us we are all connected. A shaman knows these things and more, and protects the interests of all creatures, for she knows that anything that is devastating for our animal friends is bad for human beings, too.*

## You Will Need

- ½ yard of fabric for body of bag
- ½ yard of contrasting fabric for lining
- 12" x 12" square of velvet for bag-front appliqué
- Material for template
- Sharp scissors
- 1½ yards of ribbon or decorative cord for front trim and strap
- Small scrap of microsuede cloth, soft leather, or suede for fold-over flap appliqué
- Strong, sharp needle (e.g., glove and leather needle)
- Heavyweight thread (e.g., carpet and button thread)
- Charms and/or embellishments for fold-over flap

## Assembly

### Step 1

Use the pattern on page 80 to make templates for the bag front, the bag back with fold-over flap, and the bag-front appliqué. Use the bag-front template to cut one piece from the outer-bag fabric and one piece from the lining fabric. Use the bag-back template to cut one piece from the outer-bag fabric and one piece from the lining fabric. Use the bag-front appliqué template to cut one piece from the 12" velvet square.

## Step 2

Machine stitch the bag-front appliqué to the outer-bag front.

## Step 3

Cut an 18" length from the ribbon or cord. Starting at the top corner of the bag front, machine stitch the ribbon or cord so that it covers the side and bottom raw edges of the bag front appliqué. Don't pin the ribbon or cord; just ease it gently around the curves as you sew. Trim to fit.

## Step 4

Cut a circle freehand from the scrap of microsuede cloth, soft leather, or suede for the fold-over-flap appliqué.

## Step 5

Place the outer-bag back piece right side up with the flap area at the top. Machine stitch the fold-over-flap appliqué to the flap.

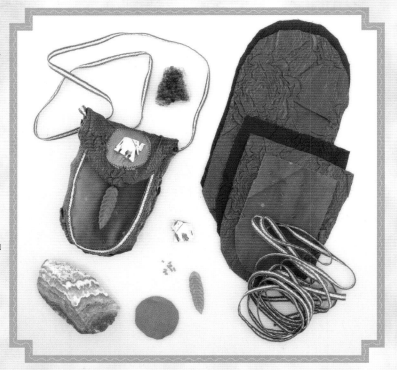

*Millions of years of conditioning have produced astoundingly refined senses in our animal brothers and sisters, especially in the realm of intuition. If we had the natural grace, self-acceptance, and instinctual abilities of the animal world and were able to merge it with the love and compassion that is our highest expression, each of us would create worlds of wonder, rich with meaning and delight.*

*Your personal medicine bag should reflect your own unique qualities and tastes. Ideally, it should help to empower your goals and aspirations. A Healing Crystal Medicine Bag made with your own hands and vision contains your love more than any commercially made item ever could. Creating a medicine bag reinforces a desired goal or experience.*

### Step 6
Place the outer-bag back piece and the lining back piece right sides together and machine stitch around the outside edges using a ⅝" seam allowance. Leave a 2" opening for turning.

### Step 7
Turn the outer bag/lining back piece right side out and stitch the 2" opening closed.

### Step 8
Repeat Steps 6 and 7 using the outer-bag front piece and the lining front piece.

### Step 9
Place the bag front and back together with the lining sides out, aligning the bottom edges. Machine stitch the pieces together along the side and bottom edges using a ⅝" seam. Leave the top edge of the bag open.

### Step 10
Turn the bag right side out and use a strong, sharp needle and heavyweight thread to hand sew the charms and/or other embellishments to the front flap.

### Step 11
Machine or hand stitch the ends of the remaining ribbon or cording to the top corners of the bag to make the strap.

PATTERN: Animal Power Medicine Bag

Enlarge 134%

BAG FRONT APPLIQUÉ
Cut 1.

⅝" seam allowance

⅝" seam allowance

fold line

BAG FRONT
Cut 1 each from outer bag
fabric and lining.

BAG BACK
Cut 1 each from
outer bag fabric
and lining.

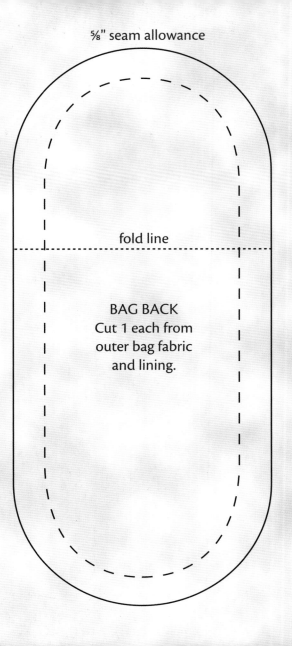

# Enchanted Collage Medicine Bag

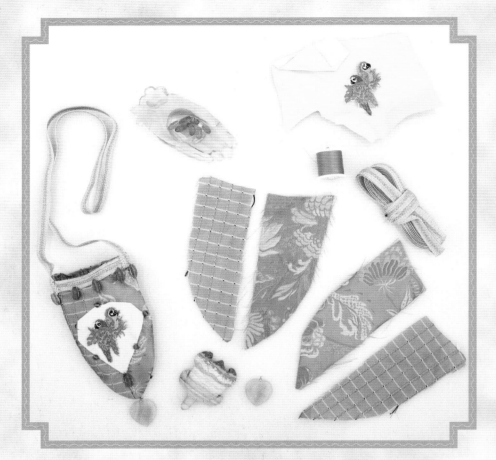

Color is vibration, the basic energy form underlying all of creation. Color is an essential ingredient in our daily environment. Not only does it communicate emotion and create a mood, but it also has the power to affect our energy levels.

# You Will Need

- ¼ yard each of two fabrics for outer bag

- ½ yard of contrasting fabric for lining

- Material for template

- Sharp scissors

- Small irregularly shaped scrap of microsuede cloth, soft leather, or suede for bag-front appliqué

- Animal patch or appliqué

- Strong, sharp needle (e.g., glove and leather needle)

- Heavyweight thread (e.g., carpet and button thread)

- Beading thread

- Size 10 beading needle

- Assorted beads and charms

- 1½ yards of braided cord for strap

# Assembly

### Step 1
Use the (half) pattern on page 85 to make a template for the outer bag. Use the template to cut two pieces from one outer-bag fabric. Reverse the template and cut two pieces from the other outer-bag fabric.

### Step 2
Use the (full) pattern on page 85 to make a template for the lining. Use this template to cut two pieces from the lining fabric, one for the front lining and one for the back lining.

### Step 3
With right sides together, machine stitch one of each outer-bag fabric pieces (not the lining) together along the center seam using a ⅝" seam allowance. Make two, one for the front of the bag and one for the back of the bag.

### Step 4
Center the irregularly shaped microsuede, soft leather, or suede scrap on the bag front. Stitch the animal patch or appliqué to the scrap, either by machine or by hand using a strong, sharp needle and heavyweight thread. If you wish, add stitching around the edges of the scrap as well.

*Seeing a color and experiencing a color are virtually inseparable, since much of what is seen is also felt. People react to colors in various ways, since they evoke personal emotions and experiences.*

### Step 5
Use beading thread and a size 10 beading needle to add beads randomly around the edges of the scrap for embellishment.

### Step 6
Pin the right sides of the outer-bag front and back pieces together and machine sew around the side and bottom edges using a ⅝" seam allowance. Leave the top edge of the bag open. Turn the bag right side out.

### Step 7
Pin the right sides of the front and back lining pieces together and machine sew around the side and bottom edges using a ⅝" seam allowance. Leave the top edge of the lining open. Do not turn the lining.

### Step 8
Insert the lining into the outer bag. Machine stitch close to the raw edge all around the top edge of the bag, using the braided cord to cover the edge, and trimming the cord to fit.

### Step 9
Use the sharp needle and heavyweight thread to hand stitch additional beads and/or charms to the bag as desired.

### Step 10
Machine or hand stitch the ends of the remaining braided cord to the top corners of the bag to make the strap.

PATTERN: **Enchanted Collage Medicine Bag**

Enlarge 147%

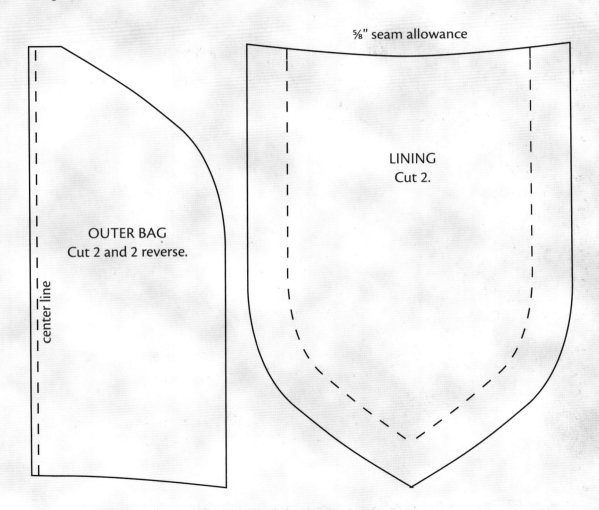

⅝" seam allowance

LINING
Cut 2.

OUTER BAG
Cut 2 and 2 reverse.

center line

# Shaman's Magic Medicine Bag

*The shamanic forces of the mind and planet can be harnessed for the service of wisdom and compassion, each tradition enhanced by the perspectives and methods of the other.*

—His Holiness, the Dalai Lama

## You Will Need

- 12" x 12" square of microsuede cloth, soft leather, or suede for body of bag
- Two small scraps of contrasting leather for circle and heart appliqués
- Material for template
- Sharp scissors and/or leather shears
- Jewelry or leather cement
- Strong, sharp needle (e.g., glove and leather needle)
- Linen cord
- Assorted charms for bag front and fold-over flap
- Leather hole punch
- Six to eight beads
- 1 yard of braided cord for strap

# Assembly

## Step 1

Use the pattern on page 90 to make templates for the bag front, the bag back with fold-over flap, the circle appliqué, and the heart appliqué. Use the appropriate templates to cut the front and back of the bag from the microsuede cloth, soft leather, or suede. Use the appropriate templates to cut a circle appliqué from one contrasting leather scrap and a heart appliqué from the other scrap.

## Step 2

Use jewelry or leather cement to attach the circle and heart appliqués to the bag front, centering them close to the bottom edge.

## Step 3

Place the wrong sides of the bag front and back pieces together, aligning the bottom edges. Use a strong, sharp needle, linen cord, and the whipstitch to hand sew the pieces together along the side and bottom edges. Whipstitching is a simple stitch that creates a diagonal pass over the edge (see photo of sample bag).

## Step 4

Using the pattern as a guide, cut fringe in the top edge of the bag back with sharp scissors or leather shears. Fold down the fringed fold-over flap.

## Step 5

Attach the assorted charms to the bag front and fold-over flap either by hand with the needle and the linen cord, or with jewelry or leather cement.

## Step 6

Cut two short lengths of the linen cord. String three or four beads onto each cord, spacing the beads evenly and tying a knot after each bead to keep it in place.

## Step 7

Using a leather hole punch, make a hole on each side of the bag back, just above the whipstitches. Insert one end of the remaining braided cord and one set of strung beads into each hole, and tie firmly.

PATTERN: Shaman's Magic Medicine Bag

Enlarge 150%

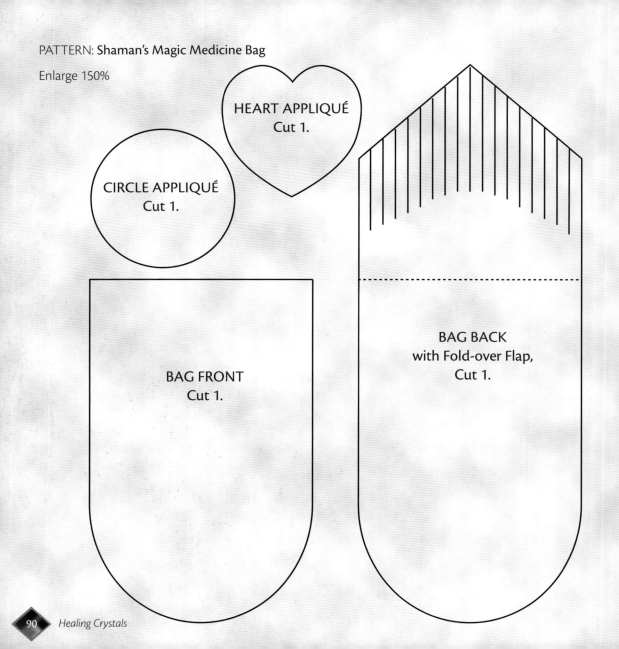

HEART APPLIQUÉ
Cut 1.

CIRCLE APPLIQUÉ
Cut 1.

BAG BACK
with Fold-over Flap,
Cut 1.

BAG FRONT
Cut 1.

# Blessed Be Medicine Bag

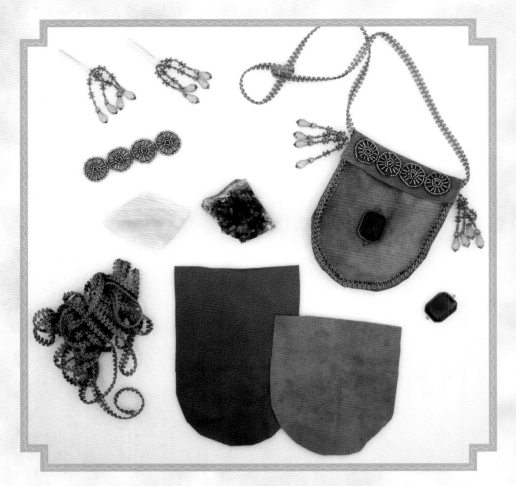

The key to choosing crystals and stones is to use your intuition. You may feel a shiver or an "aha" moment when you hold the crystal that is right for you. Remember, too, that a stone that wants to be with you will resonate with you.

## You Will Need

- 12" x 12" square of microsuede cloth, soft leather, or suede for body of bag

- Material for template

- Sharp scissors and/or leather shears

- Strong, sharp needle (e.g., glove and leather needle)

- Waxed cotton thread or linen cord

- Gemstone or cabochon for bag front

- ½ yards of braided cord for trim and strap

- Beaded embellishments for fold-over flap

- Assorted beads or ready-made beaded tassels

- Jewelry or leather cement (optional)

## Assembly

### Step 1

Use the pattern on page 95 to make templates for the bag front and the bag back with fold-over flap. Use each template to cut one piece from the microsuede, soft leather, or suede.

### Step 2

Attach the gemstone or cabochon to the bag front either by hand with a strong, sharp needle and waxed cotton thread or linen cord, or with jewelry or leather cement.

### Step 3

Place the wrong sides of the bag front and back pieces together, aligning the bottom edges. Machine stitch the pieces together along the side and bottom edges using a ¼" seam allowance. Leave the top edge of the bag open.

### Step 4

Starting at the top corner of the bag front, machine stitch the braided cord so that it covers the stitching you did in Step 3. Don't pin the cord; just ease it gently around the curves as you sew. Trim to fit.

### Step 5

Fold down the fold-over flap. Use the needle and the waxed thread or linen cord to hand stitch the beaded embellishments to the flap.

*Your personal medicine bag should reflect your own unique qualities and tastes. Ideally, it should help to empower your goals and aspirations. A Healing Crystal Medicine Bag made with your own hands and vision contains your love more than any commercially made item ever could. Creating a medicine bag reinforces a desired goal or experience.*

### Step 6

Machine or hand stitch the ends of the remaining braided cord to the top corners of the bag to make the strap.

### Step 7

Using the needle and the waxed thread or linen cord, string several lengths of beads and secure them to the corners of the bag, where the cord trim begins and ends. If you prefer, use ready-made beaded tassels.

PATTERN: **Blessed Be Medicine Bag**

Enlarge 155%

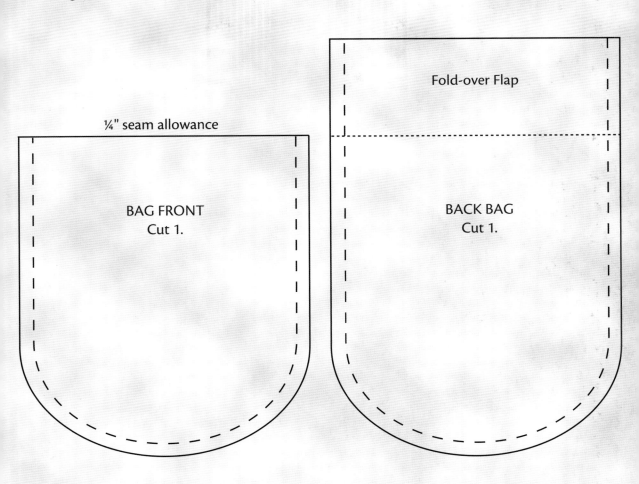

¼" seam allowance

BAG FRONT
Cut 1.

Fold-over Flap

BACK BAG
Cut 1.

# Bead-Dazzled Medicine Bag

As you sort through your materials to make your selections, repeat the intention word in your mind, and you will be guided to select appropriately. Set aside anything that you feel complements your theme: a certain color of fabric, a perfect ribbon, a silver bead.

# You Will Need

- 12" x 12" square of soft leather or pleather for body of bag
- Material for template
- Sharp scissors and/or leather shears
- Charm, medallion, gemstone, or cabochon for bag front
- Waxed cotton thread or linen cord
- Strong, sharp needle (e.g., glove and leather needle)
- Leather hole punch
- 2 yards of leather lace for drawstring and strap
- Assorted large beads for drawstrings and strap; make sure beads have large enough holes to accommodate the leather lace
- Assorted beads or ready-made beaded tassels
- Jewelry or leather cement (optional)

# Assembly

### Step 1

Use the pattern on page 100 to make a template. Use the template to cut two pieces from the soft leather or pleather. You will use one piece for the front of the bag and one for the back of the bag.

### Step 2

Attach the charm, medallion, gemstone, or cabochon to the bag front either by hand with a strong, sharp needle and waxed cotton thread or linen cord, or with jewelry or leather cement.

### Step 3

• Place the wrong sides of the bag front and back pieces together. Use the needle, the waxed thread or linen cord, and the blanket stitch to hand sew the pieces together around the side and bottom edges. Leave the top edge of the bag open.

• Thread the needle and knot the thread.

• Bring your knot to the back side of the fabric, anchoring the thread so the needle will come out of the fabric on the edge.

• Place the needle in the inner area of the blanket stitch, bringing the point of the needle out at the edge of the fabric.

• Loop the thread behind the point of the needle.

• Pull the needle through the fabric, allowing the edge thread to loop on the edge of the fabric.

• Repeat to continue sewing the edge you want covered with a blanket stitch.

- The depth of the stitch into the fabric and the spacing between stitches are important to provide a uniform blanket stitch. (See photo of sample bag.)

### Step 4
Using a leather hole punch, make eight evenly spaced holes around the top edge of the bag for the drawstring.

### Step 5
Cut two 8" lengths of the leather lace. Thread one length of lace through the holes in the front of the bag and the other through the holes in the back of the bag.

### Step 6
Thread one end of both the front and back drawstrings on one side of the bag through a large bead. Push the bead so it sits snugly against the body of the bag. Repeat for the ends on the other side of the bag.

### Step 7
Make a knot approximately 1" from the end of each individual drawstring. Thread another large bead onto the drawstring and secure with a second knot.

### Step 8
Using a leather hole punch, make a hole at the top corners of the bag, above the drawstrings. Insert the ends of the remaining leather lace into the holes and tie firmly to make the strap.

### Step 9
Hold the strap taut to find the midpoint, and then cut the strap into two equal lengths. Knot the straps together approximately 2" from the cut ends. Thread a large bead onto each cut end, securing each bead with a knot on either side.

### Step 10
Using the needle and the waxed thread or linen cord, string several lengths of beads and secure them to the corners of the bag. If you prefer, use ready-made beaded tassels.

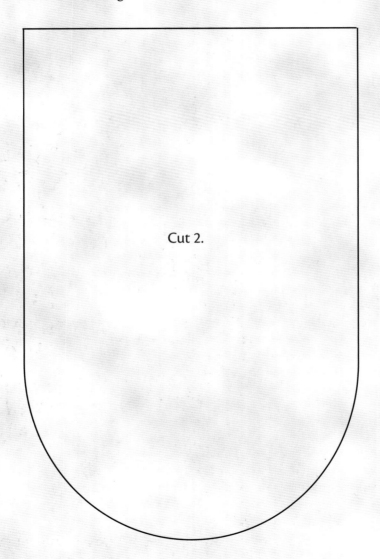

Cut 2.

# Spirit Speaks
# Medicine Bag

## You Will Need

- 12" x 12" square of microsuede cloth, soft leather, or suede for body of bag
- Material for template
- Sharp scissors and/or leather shears
- Strong, sharp needle (e.g., glove and leather needle)
- Heavyweight thread (e.g., carpet and button thread)
- Charm or beaded embellishment for bag front
- 2" x 2" square of contrasting leather for bag-front appliqué
- Waxed cotton thread or linen cord
- Jewelry or leather cement
- 1 yard of leather lace for bead-and-feather embellishment and drawstring
- Four large beads
- Feather
- Leather hole punch

## Assembly

### Step 1

Use the pattern on page 105 to make a template. Use the template to cut two pieces from the microsuede cloth, soft leather, or suede. You will use one piece for the front of the bag and one piece for the back of the bag.

### Step 2

Attach the charm or other embellishment to the 2" square of contrasting leather either by hand with a strong, sharp needle and waxed cotton thread or linen cord, or with jewelry or leather cement.

### Step 3

Use jewelry or leather cement to attach the embellished leather appliqué to the center of the bag front.

### Step 4

Cut a 2" length of the leather lace. Thread two large beads onto the lace, leaving a ¼" tail on one end. Attach a feather to the opposite end of the lace with a dot of jewelry or leather cement. You may need to trim the lace to position the feather flush with the bottom bead.

### Step 5

Center the lace tail on the bottom edge of the wrong side of the bag back. Make sure that the first bead is just a hair outside the bottom raw edge. Secure the lace tail with a dot of jewelry or leather cement.

*Your Higher Self is the part of you that knows you better than anyone else—knows your strengths and your weaknesses, your likes and dislikes, and your past and future, too. It's where your hunches, intuitions, prophetic dreams, and solutions to seemingly unsolvable problems come from. You can think of your Higher Self as the essence of your spirit, the part of you that exists beyond your physical body, beyond space and time. Your Higher Self is connected directly to God/Goddess, All There Is, or, as the Native Americans so beautifully put it, the Great Mystery.*

### Step 6

Place the wrong sides of the bag front and back pieces together. Machine stitch all around the side and bottom edges using a ¼" seam allowance and catching the lace tail in the stitches. Leave the top edge of the bag open.

### Step 7

Using a leather hole punch, make eight evenly spaced holes around the top edge of the bag for the drawstring.

### Step 8

Thread the remaining leather lace through the holes, finishing each tail with a knot 2" from the end of the lace to make the drawstring. Tie a remaining large bead to each tail.

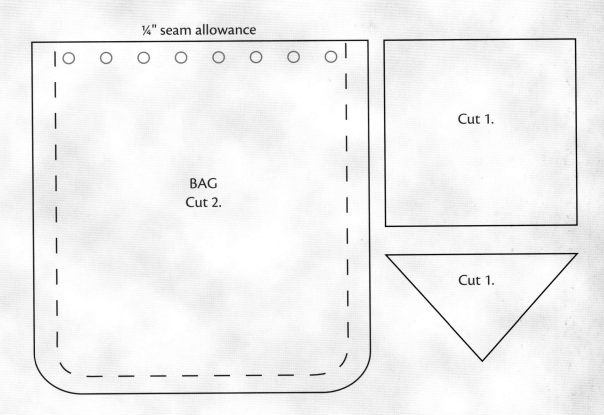

¼" seam allowance

BAG
Cut 2.

Cut 1.

Cut 1.

# Sacred Threads Medicine Bag

*Your Healing Crystal Medicine Bag can help provide a strong foundation for your spiritual journey. Working with your crystals enables you to heal and transform with ever-increasing ease and clarity. When you carry and use your Healing Crystal Medicine Bag, it embodies and reflects your intentions and the energies of your spirit and of Mother Earth.*

## You Will Need

- 12" x 12" square of microsuede cloth, soft leather, or suede for body of bag
- Material for template
- Sharp scissors and/or leather shears
- Purchased decorative appliqué
- Two 4" pieces of beaded or fringed trim
- Pins
- Jewelry or leather cement
- One round embellishment for fold-over flap; I used an antique *I-Ching* coin, but you can use whatever interesting round embellishment you wish
- 1 yard of silk cord for strap

## Assembly

### Step 1

Use the pattern on page 110 to make a template. Use the template to cut the body of the bag from the microsuede cloth, soft leather, or suede.

### Step 2

Place the body of the bag wrong side up. Fold up the bottom edge 4" to make the bag front, and crease to create the bottom fold. Unfold so that the body of the bag is right side up and the bottom crease is toward the top. Center the purchased appliqué on the bag front, just above the bottom crease. Machine stitch the appliqué in place.

*Everything in the universe is connected but unfolds in perfect divine order. Do not be attached to a time factor or to a particular way for your goal to be realized. Allow your desires to unfold in the perfect time and manner. When we have expectations and become attached to them, we can block the natural flow of energy. Often you will receive something even better or more appropriate than what you imagined and visualized in your mind.*

### Step 3

Once again, position the bag right side up with the appliquéd bag front at the top. Align the raw edge of one piece of beaded or fringed trim with one side of the raw edge of the bag front. Pin in place. Repeat to pin the remaining piece of trim to the opposite-side edge of the bag front.

### Step 4

Refold the bag body along the bottom crease, this time with right sides together. (The beaded or fringed trim will be on the inside.) Machine stitch the side seams using a ¼" seam allowance. Turn the bag front side out.

### Step 5

Fold down the fold-over flap and use sharp scissors or leather shears to cut a wavy, uneven edge.

### Step 6

Use jewelry or leather cement to attach the round embellishment to the center of the fold-over flap, close to the wavy cut edge.

### Step 7

Machine or hand stitch the ends of the silk cord to the top corners of the bag (under the flap) to make the strap.

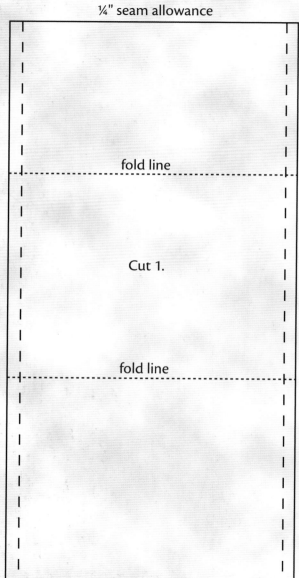

PATTERN: **Sacred Threads Medicine Bag**

Enlarge 182%

¼" seam allowance

fold line

Cut 1.

fold line

# Soul-Keeper Medicine Bag

Be patient—that is a master habit that heals. Be patient with yourself, with others, and with the invisible forces that surround and sustain you. Even your guardian spirits need time to work their miracles.

## You Will Need

- ½ yard of silk for body of bag
- ½ yard of fabric for lining
- Material for template
- Sharp scissors
- Sewing thread to match color of silk
- 2" of fine cord or braid for button loop
- Silk pins
- Strong, sharp needle (e.g., glove and leather needle)
- Heavyweight thread (e.g., carpet and button thread)
- Six 1"-long decorative beads for fold-over flap
- Button for closure
- 1 yard of silk cord for strap

## Assembly

### Step 1
Use the pattern on page 115 to make a template. Use the template to cut two pieces: one from the silk for the body of the bag and one from the lining fabric.

### Step 2
Place the right sides of the outer bag and the lining together and machine stitch around the outside edges using a ⅝" seam allowance. Leave a 2" opening at the top center for turning.

### Step 3
Turn the bag right side out. With the lining side in, fold up the bottom edge of the bag 3½" to make the bag front. Using thread to match the silk, machine stitch the sides of the bag, close to the raw edges.

### Step 4
Fold down the top of the bag, lining side in, to form a fold-over flap.

### Step 5
Use the 2" of fine cord or braid to make a button loop. Insert the raw edges of the loop into the 2" center opening in the flap. Pin, and then secure the loop by carefully machine stitching close to the edge of the flap.

Sit in a comfortable position. Imagine that you are a tree. Send roots down through your feet to the center of the Earth. Attach your roots deep into the Earth, and draw its vibrant growing energy up through your feet, and up your body through the top of your head as a spray of light radiating through and out of you like branches. Continue to draw the light energy up and around and down again in a circle of vitality. After three times, open your eyes.

### Step 6
Using a strong, sharp needle and heavyweight thread, hand stitch the six 1"-long decorative beads across the edge of the flap, just above the stitching.

### Step 7
Use the same needle and thread to stitch the button to the bag front using the button loop as a placement guide.

### Step 8
Machine or hand stitch the ends of the silk cord to the top corners of the bag (under the flap) to make the strap.

PATTERN: **Soul Keeper Medicine Bag**

Enlarge 200%

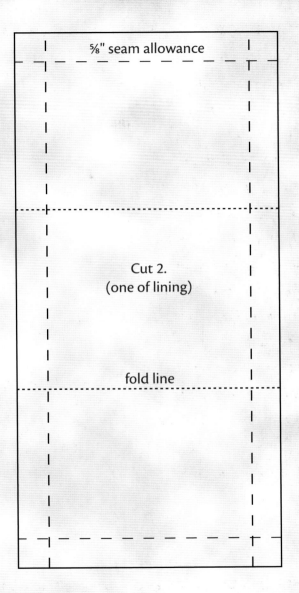

⅝" seam allowance

Cut 2.
(one of lining)

fold line

# Ancient Future Medicine Bag

*Much of what you see all around you is a physical manifestation or creation of your internal thought processes and the vibes of those who share your space. If what you see around you gives you feelings of anger, depression, or resentment, use those feelings as your guide to make changes for the better.*

## You Will Need

- 12" x 12" square of microsuede cloth, soft leather, or suede for body of bag
- Scrap of contrasting leather for bag-front appliqué
- Material for template
- Sharp scissors and/or leather shears
- Jewelry or leather cement
- Large scarab or gemstone for the bag front
- Beading thread
- Size 10 beading needle
- Assorted beads to equal 24" when strung for strap
- Assorted beads for beaded fringe

## Assembly

### Step 1

Use the pattern on page 120 to make templates for the bag and for the oval appliqué. Use the bag template to cut two pieces from the microsuede cloth, soft leather, or suede. You will use one piece for the front of the bag and one piece for the back of the bag. Use the oval template to cut one piece from the scrap of contrasting leather.

*The future belongs to those who believe in the beauty of their dreams.*

—Eleanor Roosevelt

### Step 2

Use jewelry or leather cement to attach the oval appliqué to the center of the bag front. Use the cement to attach the large scarab or gemstone embellishment to your medicine bag.

### Step 3

Place the wrong sides of the bag front and back pieces together. Machine stitch the side and bottom edges of the bag together using a ¼" seam allowance. Leave the top edge of the bag open.

### Step 4

Use beading thread and a size 10 beading needle to string a 24" length of assorted beads for the strap.

### Step 5

Securely hand stitch the ends of the beaded strap to the top corners of the bag.

### Step 6

Using the beading thread and beading needle, string five separate 1" lengths of assorted beads. Stitch these to the bottom edge of the oval appliqué to create beaded "fringe."

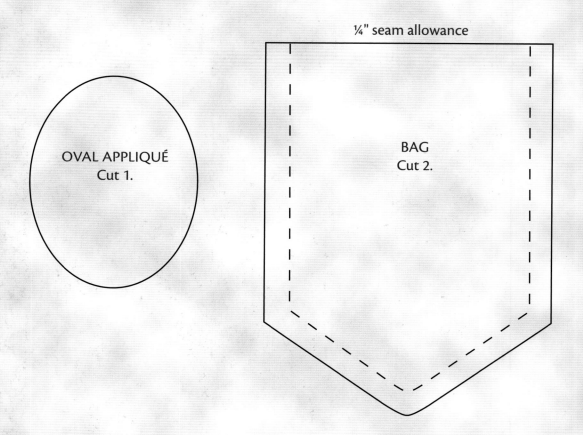

OVAL APPLIQUÉ
Cut 1.

¼" seam allowance

BAG
Cut 2.

# Messenger Medicine Bag

## You Will Need

- ½ yard of microsuede cloth, soft leather, or suede for body of bag
- Small, irregularly shaped scrap of contrasting leather for bag-front appliqué
- Material for template
- Sharp scissors and/or leather shears
- Jewelry or leather cement
- Strong, sharp needle (e.g., glove and leather needle)
- Waxed cotton thread or linen cord
- Charms for bag front
- 1 yard of braid or trim for edging
- Assorted beads to equal 24" when strung for strap
- Beading thread
- Size 10 beading needle
- Assorted beads or ready-made beaded fringe

## Assembly

### Step 1
Use the pattern on page 125 to make a template. Use the template to cut two pieces from the microsuede cloth, soft leather, or suede. You will use one piece for the front of the bag and one piece for the back of the bag.

### Step 2
Use jewelry or leather cement to attach the contrasting, irregularly cut leather scrap to the center of the bag front.

### Step 3
Attach the charms to the leather scrap either by hand with a strong, sharp needle and waxed cotton thread or linen cord, or with jewelry or leather cement.

### Step 4
Place the wrong sides of the bag front and back pieces together and machine stitch the pieces together along the side and bottom edges using a ¼" seam allowance. Leave the top edge of the bag open.

### Step 5
Starting at the top corner of the bag front, machine stitch the edging braid or trim so that it covers the stitching you did in Step 4. Don't pin the trim; just ease it gently around the curves as you sew. Trim to fit.

*Whenever you want to set a new goal for yourself, start by setting your intention with a clear affirmation and visualization. Take the time to become clear about what you want, but then simply declare it. Say to the universe, "Here is my goal. Make it so." Do not think you can tell the universe exactly how and when your goal will be achieved, however; you cannot.*

### Step 6

Align a length of the leftover braid or trim with the top edge of the bag front and stitch in place. (You may find it easier to hand stitch this piece so as not to catch the back of the bag.) Trim to fit.

### Step 7

Use beading thread and a size 10 beading needle to string a 24" length of beads for the strap. Hand stitch the ends of the strap securely to the upper corners of the bag.

### Step 8

Using the beading thread and beading needle, string five separate 2"–3" lengths of beads. Space them evenly around the sides and bottom of the bag, next to the trim. Hand stitch them in place. If you prefer, use ready-made beaded fringe.

¼" seam allowance

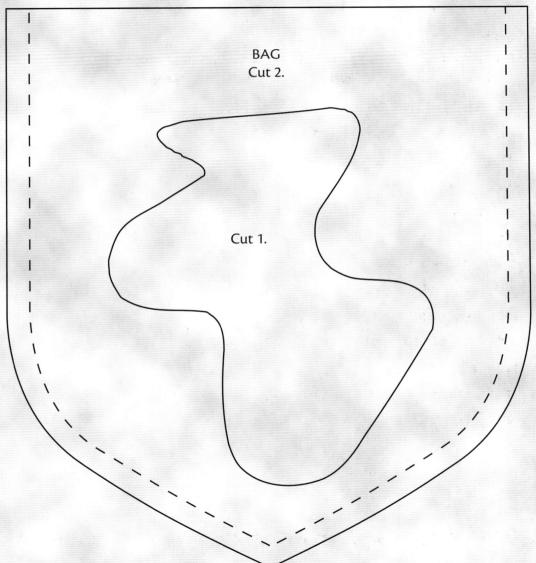

BAG
Cut 2.

Cut 1.

# Colors

When you are picking the fabrics, leathers, beads, and threads for fabricating your special medicine bag, you might want to consider the meanings of the colors to incorporate their special magic into it.

Color is vibration, the basic energy form underlying all of creation. Color is light. Color is an essential ingredient in our daily environment. Not only does it communicate emotion and create a mood, but it also has the power to affect the energy level of those of us fortunate enough to be able to see. In this way seeing a color and experiencing a color are virtually inseparable, since much of what is seen is also felt. People react to colors in various ways, since they evoke personal emotions and experiences.

You can meditate upon a specific color and carry it with you in the form of your medicine bag, your stones and crystals, or something you wear, in order to get a benefit from it. Clear your mind, take a few deep breaths, and stare at the color you have chosen. Breathe in the color until you can feel it seep into your skin and deep inside you. Repeat this ritual whenever you feel as if you need a psychic "color infusion" in order to bring healing, happiness, prosperity, or any other good thing into your life.

Following is a guide of color attributes.

# Red

Red signifies the attributes of confidence and courage. It inspires boldness in thought and deed. There can sometimes be so much passion in its energy that when it is displayed it can be perceived as aggression. When the color presents itself in a seemingly coincidental context, it can be the equivalent of a stop sign from the universe. Because of its strong psychic saturation, it needs to be used carefully, especially in a domestic environment, and in combination with a balance of other colors. Also, too much red in the environment can cause feelings of anger, irritability, or impatience.

# Fuchsia

The color fuchsia can influence both physical and spiritual well-being. It is the flag for nonconformist, innovative, strong-willed, imaginative, artistic, and creative individuals. It has the qualities of red, plus empathy; it is a mixture of passion and compassion. The negative side of its color influence is that it can create a lazy, laid-back attitude that shuns challenges and responsibilities. For this reason, people who are chronically depressed or introverted should avoid this color. Fuchsia is ideal for rituals to secure ambitions and financial rewards.

# Orange

Orange is a joyous color, representing vibrant energy and intellectual curiosity. It is the color of surprise and enthusiasm. It promotes physical attraction as well as friendship. Because orange is the color of communication, it works as an emotional and intellectual stimulant, which alleviates feelings of self-pity, lack of self-worth, and an unwillingness to forgive. It connects us to our senses and helps to remove inhibitions in order to make us independent and social. Unlike many colors, it has a sense of humor; wearing just a bit of orange can bring smiles and a sense of optimism.

# Yellow

The color yellow signifies cheerfulness, optimism, and bright ideas. Like orange, it is a happy and energetic color that reflects mental acuity and communication. It is also a celebration of sunny days. Yellow energy is related to the ability to perceive and understand, while also acting on the senses as a stimulant. It signifies the intellectual side of our nature and relates to matters of travel, information, and self-expression. Because of this, it helps in the powers of discernment and memory, decision making, and the thought process.

## Green

In the material sense green represents employment, money, prosperity, and success. In the magical sense it symbolizes fertility, healing, growth, and the good green Earth. Its strong affinity to nature helps us connect with empathy to others and to the natural world. Like plants and trees that promote wellness by putting out oxygen, green suffuses the environment with healing vibrations that give a general sense of happiness and wellness. The color connects us to unconditional love and is used to balance our whole being. Green in the aura suggests an individual who has the natural gift of healing.

## Blue

Although it is identified with feelings of sadness (the blues), this color actually promotes calm and restfulness. Blue symbolizes peace and emotional tranquility. It also inspires mental control, creativity, and clarity. Because its energy is secure and nonthreatening, it is particularly helpful in creating a soothing sleep environment for young children and insomniacs. Blue is known to have a pacifying effect. Holistic healers often treat headaches and other complaints with color therapy, using various shades of the color blue. It symbolizes

the sky, the shielding dome above our heads, and therefore represents boundless potential and opportunities.

## Aqua

Aqua is a serene yet uplifting color, balanced at a point between blue and green. Like blue, of which it is a variant, aqua has a deeply soothing quality, suggesting the beauty and serenity of a tropical lagoon. Like green, it is highly symbolic of nature. This laid-back energy is associated with meditation, sensitivity, and emotional vulnerability. Because of its association with the throat chakra, aqua promotes clear communication, honesty, openness, and the need to join with others. It represents the ability to transform, just as water turns to ice and the cycle repeats.

## Purple

Purple denotes power, authority, and psychic strength. It has been associated with royalty since classical antiquity and throughout the Middle Ages, when it was the color of choice for monarchs' ceremonial clothing. It can also infer wealth (burn to the purple). In a metaphysical sense, purple energy connects us to our spiritual guidance, wisdom, and inner strength. It is a color of artists, mystics, and fantasy seekers, so those attracted and attuned to it need to guard against living in a fantasy world. On a deeper level, purple is a color of transformation, combating fear and resistance to change.

# Indigo

Indigo is the color of spiritual awakening and awareness. It is an imaginative, intuitive, and mystical shade. Indigo is connected with artistic and musical impulses. It inspires sensitivity to beauty, harmony, and compassion for others, as well as promoting lucid dreams and dream skills such as problem solving. Indigo acts as a psychic and spiritual barrier to the ego, and it channels energy in a positive way. Indigo energy strengthens intuition and connects us to a higher spiritual realm. Its subtle vibration can be useful in ESP such as telepathy, clairvoyance, and even astral projection.

# Brown

Brown is the ultimate earth tone, reflective of nature, especially in the autumnal months. Because it is one of the most prominent colors in nature, it can be a stabilizing influence both psychologically and emotionally. It denotes practicality, simplicity, humility, and purposefulness. A wood-paneled study gives the user a sense of being ensconced in a safe, traditional, and protective environment, suggesting that brown need not be dismissed as drab or uninteresting.

# Lavender

Lavender is the color of spiritual healing, dispelling sadness, loneliness, and mental confusion. It is helpful in opening the third eye and clearing away the karmic debris from past lifetimes. On the material level, it is known as a shade of refinement and delicacy. Like pink, it is associated with femininity. It can also reflect romance, sentimentality, or old age, especially in women. Like the plant for which it is named, this gentle shade is helpful in treating bronchial and digestive disorders. It is a good color for use on a ceremonial altar or in a room where meditation or rituals are practiced.

# Pink

Pink is the color of overwhelming joy and personal happiness. It is emblematic of good health (in the pink). This lively yet gentle shade reflects optimism, a youthful attitude, and the ability to take chances. It signifies romantic rather than sexual love. It is generally associated with femininity. Pink suggests a talent for fun and the ability to bring a fresh perspective to any endeavor.

## Black

Black is not actually a color but the absence of color; it is also perceived as the combination of all colors. It can be off-putting because of its intensity, but it is actually comforting, protective, and mysterious. It is associated with silence, the void, the infinite, and the depth of outer space and beyond. For those under psychic attack, it provides a powerful shield. On the practical level, black represents seriousness and commitment to an idea or principle, a total absorption with a cause. It is good for banishing negativity, absorbing negativity, or fighting negativity from an outside source.

## Tan

Classic and understated, tan suggests the path of moderation and neutrality. While it may be seen as representing a conservative attitude, it should not be read as symbolic of boredom or being on the fence. Its energy signifies dependability, caring, and common sense. Tan is often considered to be a noncolor, but its very absence of pigment exudes a sense of relaxation and undemanding energy.

## Gray

Gray represents the middle ground, neither completely positive nor completely negative. Like tan, it is truly a neutral shade. Its energy suggests a void, emptiness, lack of movement and warmth, an overcast day, a rain-soaked sky, or the promise of snow. Yet it has a stabilizing effect, making vibrant colors stand out while muting their vibration. For this reason, gray is at its best when displayed in relationship to other, bolder colors. Although not a healing shade, gray is used in color therapy to absorb unwanted energy from the body. Emotionally, it symbolizes a willingness to comply, to be purposefully isolated in order to find a quiet and balancing energy.

## White

White is the emblem of innocence, purity, and peace and denotes spiritual authority. It radiates a protective and charismatic energy, which is why seekers and seers use it when meditating, as a protective shield or enveloping ball or egg shape of energy. It has strong religious significance, representing spiritual purification, virginity, baptism, and soul redemption. Throughout history and in most cultures, it has symbolized the loftiness of moral authority. It is particularly significant in rituals involving lunar energy. In color therapy, white strengthens and purifies the energy system of the body.

# CHAPTER 9
# Using Your Healing Crystal Medicine Bag

After you create your Healing Crystal Medicine Bag, it needs to be empowered and filled with your crystals and your intention. Lay all the cleaned and cleared crystals you wish to put in it, and the bag itself on a table. We like to use candlelight and put soft music on in the background. Relax and hold each crystal in your hand, close your eyes, and think about what you would like it to do, about your hopes and wishes. See Chapter 5, "How to Clear and Program Your Crystals" (page 57), and Chapter 11, "The Power of Intention and Affirmation" (page 134).

Thank each crystal and put it inside the bag. Once the bag is full, ask the Great Spirit to bless it and your wish. Then hold the medicine bag to your heart and visualize your wish as if it is already true. Feel what it feels like to have your wish be real in the present moment. Place the bag around your neck. Whenever you wear the bag, spend a little time holding it to your heart, envisioning your wishes as real in the present moment. You can also hold the bag in your hand and concentrate on what you want it to do for you or for the person you are gifting it to. Use your imagination and see the bag helping you or the person you are creating it for. Say the "Pathfinder Prayer of Protection" (page 147) and thank the animals, minerals, and plants that gave of themselves so that you could have this bag.

You can also place the medicine bag on your altar if you have one, or in a special place in your home. You will probably want to carry it with you often to draw on its power. Your medicine bag has many uses. You may use it when going on a vision quest of your own design.

You may want to change your crystals as your needs change, or have more than one medicine bag, each created for a particular purpose. Over time, as you listen to the Great Spirit inside of you and all around you, you will be guided to add new crystals to your bags or to remove some.

It is helpful to draw inspiration from ancient rituals. Many tribes have developed healing therapies using healing crystals and medicine bags. Using your medicine bag is a way to tune in deeply to your spirit wisdom for guidance and to welcome spirit support for your journey. When you intend to meditate or perform any ritual, carefully empty your medicine bag and hold and touch the various crystals to attune yourself. The strength you gain from them will put you in closer touch with the Great Spirit, enabling you to easily attract what you need and comfortably manifest your goals.

While the specifics of ritual practice with crystals vary greatly among tribes and practitioners, the basic concepts of crystal healing remain the same. Your ability to communicate with crystals will increase as you perfect these important steps.

Remember, your medicine bag is a self-care method. It is not meant to replace a licensed medical professional. The best approach to achieving wellness is a holistic approach. Your medicine bag and healing crystals are one part of the whole. Trust in your process, and if you listen with your heart, you will be guided correctly.

**Step 1**

Become aware of the Higher Power in the universe that is called by many names. We use the term Great Spirit, but you should use whatever name you feel most comfortable with—Goddess, God, All There Is, the Great Mystery. It is completely up to you. Allow yourself to feel the presence of that power within you.

**Step 2**

Hold your medicine bag and clarify your intentions before working on yourself or others. Clean and clear your own space and energy field. Pray and meditate to balance and strengthen yourself. Meditation will center your energy and clear your mind.

**Step 3**

Take your crystals out of your medicine bag. Talk to, listen to, and commune with them. They can offer us information we sometimes cannot contact by ourselves. You must become friends with and take good care of the crystals you work with so that they can reveal their purpose to you.

**Step 4**

Crystals are our helpers. Use your intuition and psychic sense to determine which crystals to work with. You need to become aware of your needs and desires. To find healing you need to examine your wounds. Let the crystals tell you how and when to use them.

**Step 5**

Carry your medicine bag with you. If you feel someone needs a crystal, give it away. Let the crystal go if you feel someone else needs the healing energy.

# CHAPTER 10

# The Power of Intention and Affirmation

*The future belongs to those who believe in the beauty of their dreams.*

—Eleanor Roosevelt

Much of what you see all around you is a physical manifestation or creation of your internal thought processes and the vibes of those who share your space. If what you see around you gives you feelings of anger, depression, or resentment, use those feelings as your guide to make changes for the better. By using the tools in this kit along with the power of intention, you can begin to change your experiences.

If you want to achieve something, you must clear out the doubts concerning your stated goal. You cannot allow yourself the luxury of a negative thought, because those doubts will become an intention to manifest what you don't want. When you strive to be clear and confident with your intention, your goal will manifest much more easily, but when you are conflicted in your thoughts, you will manifest obstacles. What we focus on in our mind's eye is ultimately reflected back to us in our experience of reality.

Whenever you want to set a new goal for yourself, start by setting your intention with a clear affirmation and visualization. Take the time to become clear about what you want, but then simply declare it. Say to the universe, "Here is my goal. Make it so." Do not think you can tell the universe exactly how and when your goal will be achieved, however; you cannot.

We all use affirmations every day, both positive—"I can do that"—and negative—"I cannot do that because I'm too weak, dumb, fat, skinny, poor, " and so forth, or any of the hundreds of other reasons we come up with for why we aren't living the life we want and deserve. Ever since we first started living together, we have found that setting aside a time each morning for repeating positive affirmations helps to undo the effects of negative affirmations and helps us to become aware when we are lapsing into using them. As the philosopher G. I. Gurdijeff said, "When falling asleep wakes you up, you know you are making progress."

Where we put our consciousness, we put our life energy. For some people, it could be a relationship problem, money issues, wellness, or work challenges. Sometimes we want to heal areas where there are unpleasant memories. Put your consciousness into that concern, with intention and with ritual, and notice the change that happens when you do. You may want to write an affirmation and put it into your medicine bag along with healing crystals that are appropriate to enhance your affirmation.

# Sample Affirmations

*I invent creative solutions to all challenges in my life.*

*The riches of the world come to me effortlessly.*

*I am patient in the face of delay and obstacles.*

*I have all that I need to get what I want.*

*I learn from mistakes and grow wise and strong.*

*I forgive myself, and all those who are trying to grow.*

*I surround myself with beauty and positive people.*

*I deserve love and respect because I give them.*

*I enjoy exercising, eating healthy foods, and doing what is good for me.*

*I am free of pain and suffering.*

*I am attractive because I feel good about myself and others.*

*I take my time and rest, relax, and rejuvenate.*

*I am positive that I have the power to transform my life.*

*My willpower is stronger than my bad habits.*

*I appreciate all that I have and have accomplished.*

*I earn my living doing what I love.*

*I accomplish anything I put my mind to.*

*I believe in myself now, always, and in all ways.*

*I love and accept myself as a unique individual.*

*I have faith in the future I cannot see.*

*I blend intuition and logic to guide my decisions.*

*I have faith in miracles to bless and protect me.*

# Energy Flows Where Attention Goes!

The word *intention* is used in many ways. We use it in this book to mean that what we believe strongly to be true helps to shape our experience. If we intend to break a bad habit or to set a goal to improve our lives, and we believe that it is possible, then the paths and opportunities to reach our goal will open up. The reverse is also true. If you believe that making a change in your life is going to be difficult or impossible to do, then it's more likely that you will experience failure. Your patterns of negative or positive thoughts shape your reality.

Intend that your goal manifest in a manner that is for your highest good and greatest joy. This is very important, as intentions that are created out of desperation, fear of failure, or ego issues will backfire. You may get what you want, but it will disappoint you. Alternatively, you may get the exact opposite of what you want. But intentions that are genuinely made for your highest good and greatest joy tend to manifest in a positive way.

Whether you have been looking for your soul mate, respect, contentment, romance, fun, financial security, a job you love, self-esteem, and the best life possible for you, affirmations and visualizations can be an important part of your campaign to achieve your goals. As you become more self-aware from your crystal meditations, you will naturally be more conscious of that which may hold you in disharmony, and that which empowers you. Know that you can work only on yourself; you cannot force another person to heal or to change. You can help a person to connect with tools to create his or her own healing and personal spiritual evolution.

*Intent is not a thought, or an object, or a wish. Intent is what can make a man succeed when his thoughts tell him that he is defeated. It operates in spite of the warrior's indulgence. Intent is what makes him invulnerable. Intent is what sends a shaman through a wall, through space, to infinity.*

—Carlos Castaneda

*Healing Crystals*

If you would like to increase the effectiveness of intention in your own life, the eight steps below offer some guidance.

**Step 1**  **BE CLEAR**  Become clear about your intention. What would you like to get rid of in your life? What would you like to attract? Do you want to make space in your life to attract your ideal relationship? Whatever your desires, stating your clear intention can accelerate the results.

**Step 2**  **BE CONNECTED**  If you accept the premise that everything in the universe is somehow connected, even though we can't always see that connection, you then realize that you are not separate from your desire and can fully embrace it.

**Step 3**  **BE OPEN**  Do you feel you are truly worthy and that you deserve to manifest your intention? Often an intention may be blocked energetically by an underlying belief that it is not in your best interest. If the desired result hasn't appeared in your life, there may be a block to clear. Some people have a prejudice against success, thus instinctually repelling desired goals from their lives. Do you have space energetically to receive your desire? Sometimes receiving your intention may disrupt your life, and subconsciously a part of you could be repelling it. Everyone gets tested on expanding his or her ability to receive. Experience yourself receiving your intention, know that you are deserving, and create an opening of space inside of yourself for your desire to come into your life.

Imagine and experience yourself receiving your intention now. How does it feel? The more fully you associate with your intention, the better.

**Step 4**  **BE A BELIEVER**  Your thoughts shape your reality. If you don't think intention can work, it probably won't. If you don't believe that you'll be able to attract your desire, you probably won't.

**Step 5**   **BE UNATTACHED**  Everything in the universe is connected but unfolds in perfect divine order. Do not be attached to a time factor or to a particular way for your goal to be realized. Allow your desires to unfold in the perfect time and manner. When we have expectations and become attached to them, we can block the natural flow of energy. Often you will receive something even better or more appropriate than what you imagined and visualized in your mind.

**Step 6**   **BE TRUSTING**  Once you've set an intention, it's time for trust and faith to set in, but it takes practice to develop your manifesting skills to the level where you can learn to trust them. Have faith in the process, and know that the universe is working its magic. You don't need anyone's permission to do this. Practice makes perfect.

**Step 7**   **BE EMPOWERED**  Why are you able to do this? You have that power because it is a natural human gift. By not believing in yourself, you're simply saying, "Let me be powerless," and you don't even realize it. If you think or intend weakness, you manifest weakness.

**Step 8**   **BE PATIENT**  Removing or altering ingrained habits takes time and patient practice. Be patient—that is a master habit that heals. Be patient with yourself, with others, and with the invisible forces that surround and sustain you. Even your guardian spirits need time to work their miracles.

As two people who have made their mark helping people to divine their futures, we believe that it is crucially important to have great respect for your intuition and for your ability to tap into the divine within you and all things, using that connectedness to learn about your life and your future. However, you must also expect the unexpected and show respect for the unknown, especially for all that you do not know. As Paramahansa Yogananda, the great Indian sage, said, "Trust in God, but lock your car."

# CHAPTER 11

# Chakras and Gemstones

*Chakra* is the word for "wheel" or "disk" in the strange but beautiful Sanskrit language of India, one of the most ancient languages known. It is said that each word of Sanskrit conveys the actual vibrational frequency of the thing being described.

The concept of our personal "Chakras" comes from yoga and refers to a visualization of seven energy "doorways" along our spine connecting us to the universal life force. Your chakras are seven portals to the unseen realms and the interconnectedness of all things.

## Chakra Characteristics

Here are a few basic things you should know about your chakras:

### The Chakras Actually Live Right Inside You!

Your chakras are a series of seven independent swirling centers of psychic energy said to occur along your spine, starting with your first chakra, which is said to be located at the very base of your spine, and ascending in numerical order to your seventh chakra, which is said to reside at the top of your brain just below the crown of your head.

## The Chakras Are as Pretty as a Rainbow!

Each of your chakras is a different but very specific color. Your chakras are said to ascend your spine in the following order: red at your first chakra, and then orange, golden yellow, green, blue, indigo, and violet for your seventh chakra. This mirrors the progression of the colors of the rainbow, the visible vibrating energy spectrum we call "light."

## The Chakras Have a Lot of Nerve!

The exact location of the seven chakras along the spine and up to the crown of the head is said to correspond fairly accurately to the places where the greatest concentration of nerve endings gang up (appropriately called our nerve "ganglia").

## The Chakras Are "Gland" to Know You!

The location of the chakras also corresponds to the approximate location of the glands of our endocrine system.

## The Chakras Have Relations!

Each chakra is said to be related to specific processes going on in the body, such as breathing, digesting, and even sex. They are also related to specific mental and spiritual aspects of our being.

You've probably noticed that we say that the location and properties of the various chakras are "said" to occur, ascend, correspond, and be related to. Please don't be disappointed to learn that this is because the chakras are not visible to our eyes on the physical plane. The chakras are real. We've seen them in our mind's eye during meditation, and so have a lot of other people. Chakras have been seen this way by spiritual seekers for thousands of years, beginning at the time Sanskrit was developed.

Sanskrit is said to have been consciously created by "the divine beings" who lived in perfect health and had very long life spans. They had plenty of free time to do things like think up languages and discover and name the chakras and another spiritual power system known as yoga. *Yoga* is often said to mean "union" in Sanskrit, but yoga is active, not passive, and we therefore believe it is more precise to translate it as "to unite."

In Sanskrit, each and every word created to describe a person, place, or thing was designed to vibrate at the same frequency as the thing itself vibrated so that the word and what it described would resonate sympathetically and reinforce each other. So the word *yoga* is the vibration of the concept of uniting things like your mind, body, and spirit, and *chakra* is the embodiment in sound of the concept and reality of a spinning, moving wheel.

This ancient understanding of the chakras and the power of sympathetic resonance show a remarkable degree of sophisticated scientific knowledge in the people that lived thousands of years before our time. Our distant ancestors understood that we are all made up of vibrating energy, something that was not rediscovered and proved until Albert Einstein did so in the early twentieth century!

# Chakra Colors and Locations

As we mentioned briefly above, each of the chakras represents an area of our experience and is associated with a particular color and location in our bodies.

The fiery red of the first chakra, located at the base of the spine near the coccyx, is where the powerful, primal life energy of the kundalini, yet another Sanskrit word for our animal instincts for self-preservation, lies like a coiled serpent waiting to be awakened by our divinely inspired higher will so it can climb up our spine and complete the energizing and balancing of our chakras.

Next, the orange-colored second chakra is located opposite the reproductive organs and is associated with sexuality and creativity.

The golden yellow–colored third chakra is opposite the navel and is connected to our self-assertion as we shape and expand our being in the world.

The green fourth chakra is opposite the heart and connected to our ability to love and our ability to feel the love of others toward us.

The blue fifth chakra is opposite the throat and is associated with communication, knowledge, and self-expression.

The indigo sixth chakra is located in the brow at the point where many spiritual people say the third eye is located and serves to directly connect us to all other beings through compassionate, holistic thought and psychic communication.

Finally, the violet seventh crown chakra is located at the top of the brain. Besides serving as our connection to the energy of the universe, it is connected with our devotion and identification with causes and forces beyond our individual selves.

There is a fundamental "yoga" (union) connecting the practice of yoga, our seven personal chakras, and the energy of the universe. Since its beginning in the time of Sanskrit's development, practitioners of yoga have sought union on all levels. Yoga exercises combine meditation with both motion and stillness. They are designed to produce union of the body with itself and with a calm and serene mind, thereby allowing the soul to be contacted and united with the infinite energies of the universe through the mediation of our chakras. If your chakras are blocked because you are not properly breathing, eating, eliminating, thinking, or feeling, then even the infinite energies of the universe are not going to be able to enter your body and fill it with the power of pure light.

It was the most adept yogis, those who had dedicated their lives to ultimate union with the very source of creation, who first claimed to have seen in their mind's eye during the peak of their meditation these seven spinning, wheel-like vortexes of differently colored lights they called the chakras. By focusing their meditation on their chakras, they and countless other adepts since have used them as tools in their efforts to produce self-healing, contentment in all circumstances, and even exalted states of consciousness.

As our ancient ancestors knew and Einstein proved, each of us is made up of energy— the same invisible but very real energy that everything else in the universe is made up of. That is what we call the Universal Energy Field.

Amy and I believe that the chakras are the actual points of interchange for the transfer to all of us of the life-giving force that animates and sustains our physical, mental, and emotional being from the Universal Energy Field, the very source of life. The reason that the ancient yogis and you and we are all able to use our equally invisible chakras for self-improvement and self-empowerment is because our chakras are what connect the different aspects of our individual beings— our bodies with their individual parts, our minds and our spirits— to the infinite power and wisdom of the Universal Energy Field.

We are each an inseparable part of the unseen infinite energies that surround, sustain, and empower us and All There Is. Energy is what chakras are made of and what they symbolize, and since every single bit of stuff in this entire universe is made up of energy, it is that energy which animates us, which makes the flowers grow, which makes colors, sound, and form.

The cross-legged seated yoga posture most of us are familiar with is called the lotus position because in that traditional pose of meditation, it is said that we are able to see in our mind's eye the variously colored chakra lotus flowers or *padmas*, another Sanskrit word used to describe the chakras. The chakras are visualized as giving off swirling streams of energy flowing out like the petals of a lotus flower. The awakening of these metaphysical

cerebrospinal centers is one of the highest goals of the mystic, for by fully achieving this they can become, for a time, one with All There Is. The importance of the chakras may have even been known in early Christian circles based upon references made to the "mystery of the seven stars" and the "seven churches" in the Book of Revelation (1:20).

When you visualize your chakras in your mind's eye, realize that what you are seeing are the portals where the energy of the universe is flowing into your being and filling you with life, and then flowing back out again to add your contribution to the universe. The reason that using the associated chakra gemstones can have a positive effect on your body, mind, and spirit is because the chakras are nothing less than the seven portals to infinite power.

# Chakras and Their Correspondences

Following are the descriptions of the chakras in their order and the various gemstones and meanings associated with each of them.

Many people chose a specific crystal that represents the chakra they need to work on and keep it with them in their medicine bag.

The following list points out specific issues and imbalances. If you are encountering a blockage of the flow of energy, or if there is a current struggle in your life, check the list to see which chakra is connected to your issue. Then choose the gemstone to create your ritual. To heal with the crystals, simply relax and place the crystals on your body in the corresponding location of the chakra and visualize that chakra aligning its vibration with that of the crystal (see photo). You can combine the crystal healing with visualizing the chakra colors, while affirming a balancing of the issues involved.

You may also want to create a special medicine bag in the color of the chakra you are working with. You can wear the associated stone or color; by placing the bag, colors, and stones on your altar or bedside, you will enhance your intention.

## Chakra 1: RED ROOT

*Location:* groin, at the base of the spine in the area of the coccyx

*Body parts:* bones, nails, teeth, prostate, anus

*Color:* red

*Gems:* garnet, obsidian, hematite

*Musical note:* C

*Issues:* survival instincts, self-preservation, early childhood

*When this chakra is balanced:* secure, prosperous, vital

*When this chakra is imbalanced:* insecure, fearful, susceptible to illness

## Chakra 2: ORANGE CREATIVITY

*Location:* lower abdomen

*Body parts:* reproductive organs, bladder, kidneys

*Color:* orange

*Gems:* carnelian, agate

*Musical note:* D

*Issues:* sexuality, creativity, relationships

*When this chakra is balanced:* emotionally intelligent, fulfilled, sensual

*When this chakra is imbalanced:* overly sensitive, repressed, immobilized

**Chakra 3: YELLOW POWER**

*Location:* solar plexus above the navel

*Body parts:* lower back, stomach, liver, spleen, digestive system

*Color:* yellow

*Gems:* citrine, topaz, amber

*Musical note:* E

*Issues:* personal power, will, self-worth

*When this chakra is balanced:* effective, spontaneous, filled with self-esteem

*When this chakra is imbalanced:* worried, nervous, lacking purpose

 **Chakra 4: GREEN HEART**

*Location:* heart, midchest

*Body parts:* upper back, chest, skin, circulation

*Color:* green or pink

*Gems:* jade, rose quartz, malachite

*Musical note:* F

*Issues:* peace, love, forgiveness, intimacy

*When this chakra is balanced:* compassionate, empathetic, trusting

*When this chakra is imbalanced:* self-pitying, paranoid, sleepless

 **Chakra 5: BLUE THROAT**

*Location:* throat

*Body parts:* thyroid, vocal chords, neck

*Color:* blue

*Gems:* turquoise, blue lace agate

*Musical note:* G

*Issues:* communication, self-expression, faith

*When this chakra is balanced:* creative, inspired, independent, truthful

*When this chakra is imbalanced:* self-righteous, secretive, evasive

 **Chakra 6: INDIGO BROW**

*Location:* between the brows

*Body parts:* face, eyes, nose

*Color:* indigo

*Gems:* lapis, sodalite

*Musical note:* A

*Issues:* channeled guidance, archetypal symbolism, healing

*When this chakra is balanced:* open, intuitive, perceptive, deep

*When this chakra is imbalanced:* closed off, skeptical, naïve, rigid

**Chakra 7: VIOLET CROWN**

*Location:* top of head

*Body parts:* brain, skull

*Color:* violet

*Gems:* amethyst, clear quartz, opal

*Musical note:* B

*Issues:* universal awareness, spiritual knowledge, protection

*When this chakra is balanced:* understanding, devoted, generous

*When this chakra is imbalanced:* self-destructive, frustrated, lonely

# How to Work with Your Chakras and Crystals

Choose a purpose and your intention for this Healing Crystal session by determining which chakra (and corresponding crystal) you will work with.

*Example:*

**Purpose:** Today I am unblocking (or energizing) my heart chakra using malachite and the color green.

*Example:*

**Intention:** I want to be less paranoid, and more forgiving and compassionate of others.

Follow these ten steps:

*Step 1*

Choose and clear the stones(s) you want to work with.

*Step 2*

Lie down in a quiet place and get comfortable.

*Step 3*

Place your crystal(s) on the corresponding chakra area(s).

*Step 4*

Close your eyes and take several slow, deep breaths.

*Step 5*

Feel yourself relax and release the cares of the day.

*Step 6*

Visualize the color, and affirm your intention and purpose.

*Step 7*

Continue to relax by breathing deeply and slowly.

*Step 8*

Repeat your visualization and your intention.

*Step 9*

Slowly open your eyes, pick up the crystal, and slowly sit up.

*Step 10*

Feel the energy rebalanced in your body, mind, and spirit.

# CHAPTER 12

# Pathfinder Prayer of Protection

Take three slow, comfortable, deep breaths in through your nose, and let each one slowly out through your mouth. Visualize in your mind's eye a silver cord wrapping around your ankles and feet and then going down deeply into Mother Earth. This will serve to ground you during your session. Imagine a sphere of white light surrounding you. This is the white light of purification.

Repeat the prayer at right as you breathe slowly and evenly:

*Oh, Great Spirit! Creator of the universe and all things. I feel your love and protection.*

*Guide me on the path to my highest good and greatest joy.*

*I call on the Four Directions to erect an impenetrable circle of protection around us now.*

*Oh, Spirit of the North, teacher of the mysteries. I feel your love and protection.*

*Oh, Spirit of the East, teacher of beginnings. I feel your love and protection.*

*Oh, Spirit of the South, teacher of faith. I feel your love and protection.*

*Oh, Spirit of the West, teacher of endings. I feel your love and protection.*

*Oh, Spirit of the Ancestors who have come before me and know my situation well.*

*Because of your struggles I am alive. I thank you for your sacrifices. I feel your love and protection.*

*I ask for your guidance and understanding so that I may grow and learn to create a better place for those who will come after me.*

*Oh, Mother Earth, mother of us all. I release my fears, doubts, and negativity into the fire in your heart center. I feel your love and protection.*

*I thank you all for protecting me and surrounding me with your pure love and light.*

Now you are in a state of relaxed contemplation.

# CHAPTER 13

# Worry Release

Our fears are a method of self-protection born from our desire to avoid dangers from unknown or unfamiliar situations or to avoid repeating negative experiences we ourselves have had or learned about. Knowing this fact is the first step to using your fears to work for you. Remembering it is the best way to ensure that they will.

To attain the power of a vision quest, a shaman must overcome the greatest obstacle of all—the fear that dwells within every human being. A shaman does not just push fears down, though—he goes on despite having them, something we call being a hero in our culture. A true shaman concentrates every ounce of being on confronting these fears, becomes comfortably acquainted with every fear, and by so doing removes their power to impede spiritual progress. In fact, when fears are confronted they become our allies in accomplishing our goals. If this sounds confusing, remember why our fears exist in the first place: to help us!

*In the hour of adversity be not without hope. For crystal rains fall from black clouds.*

—Persian Proverb

The survival instinct is primal, lodged in what is called the "limbic" section of our brain. This is also known as our "serpent" brain because it is the most central part of our brain, at the brain stem, and it looks just like a serpent's brain. Of course, we have two more sections of our brain, which is what makes us human beings. The serpent brain is the "me first" part of our brain that exists to ensure our survival in every way. To avoid danger and possible annihilation, we will go to great lengths and even perform seemingly superhuman feats. Fear is usually what triggers these abilities.

Fear also prevents us from getting into trouble. If we were fearless, we would not last long. The world can be a dangerous place, and fear exists to help us stay safe. The problem comes when our fears stop being our servants and become our masters. This usually happens when we are tired or depressed or have lost our self-confidence for some reason. When we are feeling weak and believe we are unable to cope with what life confronts us with, our serpent brain kicks in, whether we realize it or not. Our brain starts sending out danger signals, which starts our body secreting adrenaline and a host of other chemicals to prepare us to fight or flee. We usually do not realize this is happening and so we just become agitated and irritable, and eventually our stamina becomes depleted from being in danger mode for too long.

When you are afraid, be aware of it. If you let it, your fear will tell you why it has come into being at that particular moment, but you must listen. Your fear will also teach you invaluable lessons about yourself and your beliefs about your life.

We all have certain beliefs and attitudes that can trap us and keep us from moving toward creative solutions. Wanting to know exactly how things are going to turn out, perfectionism, and worrying about what others will think can limit us because of our reluctance to let go of trying to control, not just our creative process, but our life as a whole. Fortunately, once you pinpoint your habitual anxieties and their influences in your life, you can begin to make choices about them.

Here is a quick exercise to release anxiety and to allow your intuition to guide you. If you do the following affirmation with a strong conviction, you should immediately feel the loving attention and support of the Great Spirit or whatever you choose to call the force that animates all life.

Close your eyes and breathe deeply. Feel your body relax. Breathe in through your nose while expanding your tummy, then blowing out slowly through your mouth. Do this six times. Visualize that you are a bird in a closed birdcage. You notice that the door is ajar. You can leave the cage of your own free will. Are you afraid to fly out, to be free, or is it more comfortable to stay inside?

Say these words, either out loud (if you are alone) or to yourself:

*Great Spirit, please help me. My anxieties crowd around me, seeking to trap me. Release me from their powers. Grant me the freedom to fly and let go of all traps enclosing me.*

Keep breathing deeply as you feel your spirit fly free into the light of expansion and liberation. Open your eyes and grant yourself a vacation from your worries!

# CHAPTER 14

# The Crystal Medicine Wheel

*Peace...comes within the souls of men when they realize their relationship, their oneness, with the universe and all its powers, and when they realize that at the center of the Universe dwells Wakan-Tanka, and that this center is really everywhere; it is within each of us.*

—Black Elk (Hehaka Sapa), Oglala Sioux

Black Elk's awe-inspiring shamanic understanding of the center being everywhere is one that modern quantum physicists are only now beginning to understand. This concept is incorporated into the Native American medicine wheel, a representation of all of nature. It is a wheel of protection and it is a circle that acts as a mirror, as it represents an outward expression of our inner life, a microcosm of the macrocosm. It is a mirror that helps us to see what is taking place within ourselves. It is a map to help us find our way. We can use the wheel to understand life and spirit. The medicine wheel is a symbol of balance, perfection, completeness, and wholeness. The medicine wheel exists in us all.

We see the medicine wheel as the eight directions. When we honor the medicine wheel, we honor our connection to the universe we are part of.

The medicine wheel traditionally consists of rocks that are placed in a very specific circular fashion. The energy within the wheel, especially while ceremonies are performed, is powerful. Stonehenge in England is a standing-stone medicine wheel. From our personal visit to Stonehenge, we believe this circle of stones was used for prayer, ceremony, magic, and healing.

In our own garden we created a large stone medicine wheel many years ago, and were honored to have it blessed by our dear friend the late Professor Arnold Keyserling of Vienna, Austria, a world-renowned expert in the great philosophies of the world. He led us in a beautiful ceremony, and we share, below, some information about the directions that we learned from him, a great teacher called "Grandfather Frog" by the Native Americans he loved and lived with for many years.

This process is all about your intention, and as we have learned, crystals can be programmed and charged to amplify our intentions. Focus on each direction and what meaning each one holds for you. Listen to the messages and lessons that come to you as you contemplate each stone in your wheel.

## MEDICINE WHEEL COLOR AND STONE SYMBOLISM

### North
White, wisdom of our elders, winter, quartz crystal

### East
Yellow and red, dawn, illumination, inspiration, spring, carnelian, opal, citrine

### South
Green, heart, warmth, emotions, summer, malachite

### West
Blue and black, introspection, self-examination, reflection, fall, lapis, hematite, obsidian

One can make a beautiful small medicine wheel with tumbled stones. Choose stones that suit the size of your available space.

To make your wheel, choose a level surface on a table or stand where it will not be disturbed. After choosing your crystals (you will need between nine and thirty-two), take some notes on paper to express your intentions for this wheel. Smudge or burn incense to clear the space. You can also place bowls of sea salt, flowers, and candles in this altar area that will add peace and ambience to you sacred space.

Take your clear quartz crystal and place it in the center with other crystals surrounding it in a circle. The center of the wheel is a place of peace and light, where the Great Spirit is represented. The medicine wheel is your circle of power and protection. Start with north and go around in a clockwise path to place crystals of your choice in all eight directions. You can continue to fill in the wheel with stones to make a beautiful pattern. We like to make a gradation of colors, one flowing into the other, anchored by the colors of the four basic directions.

To consecrate the space, center yourself with the Pathfinder Prayer of Protection (page 147) and gratitude for your crystals. Focus on the crystal medicine wheel and meditate with the intention of your purpose. Each time you use a crystal medicine wheel, purify the crystals and your space with smudging and prayer before you begin your meditation and requests to the directions. After your ritual, remember to close the space.

# The Eight Directions

To the unaware, the directions are simply conveniences on maps and compasses. They are taken for granted like so many things whose power and significance are no longer understood.

To shamans around the world, the Directions are second only to the Great Spirit in power and significance. No ritual can be allowed to take place unless the directions are acknowledged and asked to bless it.

Our modern-day thinking may attribute this to the obvious fact that the directions enable us to orient ourselves in space, and without them we could never find our way on any path at all. However, it must be remembered that to people whose lives are totally integrated with Mother Nature, the world is alive! The directions are living things in space, not merely points to head toward or retreat from. They have personalities, interests, and the ability to give us guidance about the areas of life they concern themselves with.

When we are born, life begins in the East. Our teenage years are in the South. Midlife is in the West, and when we reach the North, we are the elders. We go to the spirit world after we have done our many deeds on Mother Earth. The journey does not end . . . the cycle continues.

Find your own way of calling up the directions. You may want to close your eyes and use your own unique poems, and include important pictures or symbols. We have offered you our special prayers, below.

# North

The North signifies wisdom and knowledge and the ability to teach and learn from each other. It is the place of darkness and enchantment, where the long nights help us to appreciate life's mysteries. North is associated with the earth element. From the North come gifts associated with work, stability, practicality, and patience.

*Prayer:* "Spirit of the North, fill me with patience and understanding, and help me to meditate in silence. I give thanks to The Great Mystery."

# Northeast

The Northeast signifies the muses, who inspire the arts and help us ground our vision and create our own reality.

*Prayer:* "Spirits of the Northeast, inspire me to make my art a work of life and my life a work of art. I give thanks for creativity."

# East

The East signifies illumination, awakening, and enlightenment. It is the place where the sun rises each day, giving us new and renewed hope. East is associated with the air element. From the East come gifts associated with communication, freedom, and the powers of perception.

*Prayer:* "Spirit of the East, fill me with the hope of a new day and inspire me with new perceptions. I give thanks for the sunrise."

## Southeast

The Southeast signifies the spirits of the ancestors, the teachers of humanity who guide us from beyond through our practice of prayer and divination—contacting the Divine within us.

**Prayer:** "Spirit of the Southeast, help me to listen to the ancient voices who can help me discern the truth. I give thanks for the elders."

## South

The South signifies energy, self-confidence, and faith in the intuitive process. It is the place where the warm sun purifies the fire of love in our hearts. South is associated with the fire element. From the South come gifts associated with courage, passion, enthusiasm, and generosity.

**Prayer:** "Spirit of the South, fill me with passion and give me the courage to trust my intuition. I give thanks for your warmth."

## Southwest

The Southwest signifies the nature spirits—the elementals Western cultures call fairies, gnomes, trolls, and dwarves—who help us to joyfully make our dreams come true.

**Prayer:** "Spirits of the Southwest, guide me to have more fun and notice the magic in my life. I give thanks for the little things in life."

## West

The West signifies fulfillment, nurturing, and integration. It is the place of sunsets and harvests, helping us to look peacefully within ourselves. West is associated with the water element. From the West come gifts associated with introspection, forgiveness, compassion, and healing.

**Prayer:** "Spirit of the West, fill me with compassion and forgiveness, and open my heart so I may love myself and others more. I give thanks for your innocence."

## Northwest

The Northwest signifies the cosmic messengers, the angels, who protect us and ease our pain during difficult transitions.

**Prayer:** "Spirits of the Northwest, protect me on my travels and my passage through the stages of my life. I give thanks for growth."

# CHAPTER 15

# Going on a Crystal Vision Quest

A vision quest is an ancient process undertaken by medicine people and other deeply religious seekers in the indigenous societies of our world. Those going on a vision quest traditionally withdraw from everyday life to a place of solitude. Often, they fast and pray and meditate continually on the spiritual, unseen side of life. In a vision quest, the worlds between the worlds become visible. The world of dreams, the worlds of nature spirits, angels, crystals, and stones, are revealed to be as real as our normal waking consciousness.

They pray that they may actually see those usually invisible realms and directly experience the powerful forces associated with them. Tradition and experience teaches that if they can cope with the rigors of their physical circumstances and, most important, if they can persevere in the face of their own fears, they will have a waking vision in answer to their efforts. A vision quest deeply affects those who experience them, often influencing them for the rest of their lives. It is common for the visionary to carry his or her experience back to the clan as a message for all to hear and learn from.

However, few of us have the time or inclination to withdraw totally from our everyday routines, deprive ourselves of comforts, and pray without ceasing to actualize our creative aspirations. Fortunately, it is not necessary to do so.

What is necessary is to learn what your personal vision quest entails.

It is important that you try to remember that you already are on one. Furthermore, you must use your vision quest to fan your dream into your passion, and to respect yourself as both a spiritual seeker and a "shaman." A shaman is the name given to those who demonstrate the ability to contact the highest realms and bring back useful information and powers that they share with those ready to experience them.

Your vision quest does require you to withdraw somewhat from your everyday routine. Your old ways must be replaced with new habits of creative thinking and activity. Make no mistake; old habits die hard. It is as if they have a life independent of your own and your desires to change. The only way to change them is to forget about them to the degree you are currently able to do, and to spend your time thinking and acting more in keeping with your desire to actualize your creativity.

The Crystal Vision Quest is the time that you take for soul cleansing, when you plunge into deep contact with the mysteries of life, and especially of your life, while holding and meditating with your crystals as helpers. This introspection gives us recognition of the suffering that is sometimes necessary to deepen our awareness of ourselves. There are shadows to be met and sorrows and slumps to get in touch with. Do not think in terms of conquering or getting over your fears, pain, and other vulnerabilities. They are all fertile ground in which to plant the seeds of manifestation. Besides, who ever gets over such things, anyway? We learn to live with them, and that is enough.

Our vulnerabilities are callings to look within, recirculate the energy, and ground it in form. The Crystal Vision Quest is an effort to go back to the feeling of wholeness by turning inward for power. The search for this inner power is the "medicine" the shamans seek. They want that which will heal them and make them whole.

**Step 1**   Build your medicine wheel with your chosen stones. Smudge yourself for purification and consecration of the sacred space.

**Step 2**   Take a moment and focus on your intention for your vision quest.

**Step 3**   After focusing on this intention, pray to the Great Spirit, asking for blessings and vision. Ask the Great Spirit to surround and protect you.

**Step 4**   Hold your hands over your Healing Crystal Medicine Wheel. Call on the eight directions as described in Chapter 15, "The Crystal Medicine Wheel."

**Step 5**   Pray for a vision while you take some quiet, reflective time. Call on your spirit guides.

**Step 6**   Be open to the symbols and signs that come to you.

**Step 7**   Offer gratitude and close the space.

If you learn to listen to your inner voice, and conquer your fears, you will be one of the most powerful people in the world. As the ancient Chinese *Book of Tao* says, "He who conquers others is great. He who conquers himself is greatest." You cannot really conquer your fears or yourself, but you can make friends with them both. To some degree or another, your fears will always be with you, doing their best to keep you safe and secure, even if you do not want them to. Like the development of your creativity, your vision quest is, ultimately, a lifetime's work, but it's worth it. Enjoy your journey, and use your gifts!

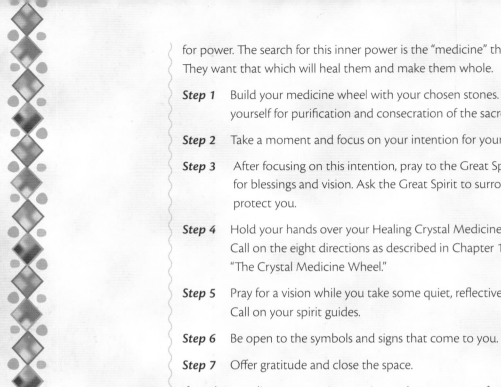

# Suggested Sources and Suppliers

### Note from the Authors

Love is the greatest tool for healing. We can use crystals to raise our personal vibration to a more loving, enchanted level, and to help clear our blocks to giving and receiving love. At all times, give thanks and show your gratitude for all that you have. Send healing energy and whatever clarity you can share out into the world. Keep your sense of humor and your sense of proportion as you seek to become yourself, fully. Put each person you meet in the center of your world and theirs. Many blessings to you, and may you seek to have contentment in all circumstances.

Always walk in beauty, for beauty walks in you.

*Amy and Monte*

We have always enjoyed looking for and finding interesting materials in thrift stores, flea markets, and appealing little rock and mineral shops. Wherever we go, we like to explore and bring back special mementos and supplies that Amy can use in her collages and illustrations. Ebay offers a vast storehouse of fabrics, ribbons, crystals, and beads. There are also many online sources, and we offer some suggestions below.

### CRYSTALS
www.wrightsrockshop.com
www.craftstones.com
www.ravencrystals.com
www.treasuresfromtheearth.net

### BEADS
www.artbeads.com
www.suncountrygems.com
www.firemountaingems.com

### LEATHER AND TOOLS
www.tandyleatherfactory.com
www.leathercordusa.com
www.brettunsvillage.com

### FABRIC
www.fashionfabricsclub.com
www.fabricmartfabrics.com
www.fabric.com
www.homesew.com

### SAGE
www.taosherb.com
www.spiritapothecary.com
www.spiritualscents.com

### TRIMS AND EMBELLISHMENTS
www.mjtrim.com
www.shop.continentalstitcherytrims.com
www.atreasurenest.com
www.trimsplus.com
www.store.wanderingbull.com

*Special Thanks*

To my mother, Jessie Spicer Zerner, Ma, a true great spirit whose animal drawings grace this book and whose loving energy graces our lives.

To Mary Jane Seely for giving us our first crystal and for helping me make the medicine bags in this book.

To our little shaman cat, Zane, who teaches us animal wisdom every day.

## About the Authors
# Monte Farber & Amy Zerner

Internationally known self-help author Monte Farber's inspiring guidance and empathic insights impact everyone he encounters. Amy Zerner's exquisite, one-of-a-kind spiritual couture creations and collaged fabric paintings exude her profound intuition and deep connection with archetypal stories and healing energies. For more than thirty years they've combined their deep love for each other with the work of inner exploration and self-discovery to build The Enchanted World of Amy Zerner and Monte Farber: books, card decks, and oracles that have helped millions answer questions, find deeper meaning, and follow their own spiritual paths.

Together they've made their love for each other a work of art and their art the work of their lives. Their best-selling titles include *The Chakra Meditation Kit*, *The Tarot Discovery Kit*, *Karma Cards*, *The Enchanted Spellboard*, *Secrets of the Fortune Bell*, *Little Reminders: Love & Relationships*, *Little Reminders: The Law of Attraction*, *Goddess, Guide Me!*, *The Animal Powers Meditation Kit*, *Astrology Gems*, *True Love Tarot*, *The Enchanted Tarot*, *The Instant Tarot Reader*, *The Psychic Circle*, *Wish upon a Star*, *The Pathfinder Psychic Talking Board*, *The Truth Fairy*, *Spirit of the Ancestors Altar Kit*, *Vibe-Away!*, *The Mystic Messenger*, *The Breathe Easy Deck*, *Tarot Secrets*, *The Healing Deck*, and *The Ghostwriter Automatic Writing Kit*.

THE ENCHANTED WORLD of AMY ZERNER & MONTE FARBER

DISCARD

Visit their popular website: www.TheEnchantedWorld.com

Or write to them at:

The Enchanted World
Box 2299
East Hampton, NY 11937
USA